D1082870

Science Speaks to Power

Science Speaks to Power

The Role of Experts in Policy Making

David Collingridge
and
Colin Reeve

St Martin's Press, New York.

© David Collingridge, 1986

All rights reserved. For information, write:
Scholarly & Reference Division,
St. Martin's Press, Inc.,
175 Fifth Avenue,
New York, NY 10010

First published in the United States of America in 1986

Printed in Great Britain

ISBN 0-312-70274-4

Library of Congress Cataloging-in-Publication Data
Collingridge, David.
  Science speaks to power.
  Bibliography: p.
  Includes indexes.
  1. Science and state.   2. Policy sciences.
I. Reeve, Colin.   II. Title.
Q125.C545   1986   338.9'26   86-3907
ISBN 0-312-70274-4

ULSON LIBRARY
NORTHERN MICHIGAN UNIVERSITY
MARQUETTE MICHIGAN 49855

To W. S. C.
From one sceptic to another

Contents

Preface

Science is being used today in ever-widening areas of policy-making, something which calls for critical scrutiny on two counts. To put the first of these bluntly: the greater the role taken by scientific experts in making decisions of a political nature, the less room is there for ordinary mortals who lack their training and qualifications. Concern for democracy should accept such a shift of power from the non-expert to the professional only if the most intense inspection reveals unequivocal advantages in terms of better decision-making. The second argument behind the present study is that scrutiny might tell us something about the intellectual status of science. Scientists can agree about the most refined and abstract theories—at least when their interests are confined to the laboratory and seminar room—but then so can theologians and astrologers. Where science appears to have the advantage over such fields of inquiry, however, is in its applications to real-world decisions involved in the development of technology and in guiding policymaking. The intellectual superiority of science is demonstrated, or so it seems, by its usefulness in the real world to hard-headed technologists, politicians and administrators. Some assessment of the intellectual standing of science may therefore be possible through an examination of its use in policymaking. These two lines of thought have come together in the present book.

There is a paradox involved in the use of scientific research in policymaking: as the complexity of their problems has increased, decision-makers have come to be ever more dependent on the results of scientific investigations, and yet it has become increasingly clear over recent years that attempting to use science in this way can generate severe problems for all concerned—policymakers and scientists alike. Science is, in reality, far from the happy servant of policy so often depicted. Typically, an actor involved in the policy process will stress the adequacy of the scientific information upon which he hopes to base his own actions, only to find that the political opposition questions the data which has been assembled and the interpretation which has been placed on it, perhaps putting forward a rival scientific case more in keeping with his own political interests. The aim was to limit political dispute by appeal to objective, scientifically established facts which no one could deny without losing all credibility as a rational agent, but instead the political debate has been widened by generating a technical argument about the data and its interpretation. As more scientific research is done in the hope of limiting the arguments, the reverse in fact occurs since there are an increasing number of technical issues under dispute. The result is embarrassment and frustration for all: policy actors feel cheated because their experts have failed to put together a watertight case, immune from the scepticism of the opposition, and the scientists are injured by what they see as the gross insensitivity of the policy process—with its deadlines and its need for clear-cut conclusions—to the finely-balanced machinery of scientific method.

Such a picture is all too common, and by now it is well documented in the literature of administration and the social studies of science, if not fully understood by the unhappy scientists and policy actors themselves. And yet science still has a fatal attraction for policymakers. Many current political controversies, for example over acid rain, lead in petrol, intelligence tests, nuclear hazards, and so on, have produced their own cottage industry of scientific research. Why does science hold such an attraction, when its use so often results in sorrow? Here we have a myth at work, and one so powerful as to be virtually irresistible. Science, when properly exercised, is supposed to yield judgements which are beyond question, whatever the political differences may be. If enough scientific research can be done, then it can be established that, for example, emissions from British power stations damage trees in Scandinavia—established so firmly that no one can oppose action to remedy the problem, although there may still, of course, be plenty of scope for purely political arguments about the best way of doing it. The reality could not be further from this myth. One of the central arguments of this book is that relevance to policy, by itself, is sufficient to completely destroy the delicate mechanisms by which scientists normally ensure that their work leads to agreement. Consensus on scientific questions which are more than marginally relevant to policy is therefore impossible. Science under these conditions leads not to agreement, but to endless technical bickering about an ever-growing number of issues.

The second argument of the book is that this failure of science to operate as smoothly as mythology would have it does not in effect matter for policymaking. Problems appear, once again, only through the influence of mythology—this time concerning the need to gather in all relevant information before a decision can be intelligently made. Not only does this demand time and money, which are generally unavailable, it places the most naïve trust in the power of science to deliver information. A more realistic view of the capabilities of science forces on us a more realistic conception of the policy process, one more closely tailored to the limitations of scientific method and of the human intellect. Incrementalism is defended in this way, for it describes a way of making policy choices which makes very small demands on scientific research. There are therefore good and bad messages for policymakers from the book. The bad news is that their problems in using science are fundamental, concerning the very nature of consensus building in science, and as such cannot be wished away by administrative reforms or by insisting upon using only unbiased, disinterested researchers. But the accompanying good news is that their problems with science are more to do with the failure of myths, about the power of science and decisionmakers' needs for information, than with any real problem. Once policymakers can admit to operating in a system where decisions have to be made in an incremental way, with little call on science, then these problems may be greatly eased.

The book's case studies, drawn largely from British and United States sources, are presented in a non-technical, straightforward way, with minimum use of jargon. They may therefore be used by students whose interests are more likely to be stimulated by a case study approach than a theoretical treatment of the material. The balance between theory and case study will, we hope, be easily adjusted to suit the needs of particular groups of students.

The clearest way to see the connection between the present work and David Collingridge's other books is through the central concept of error. If mistakes in decisions are unavoidable, there being no way to ensure their absence, it makes sense to favour choices which are flexible—ones which can be detected as erroneous early on, and which can be quickly and cheaply remedied upon discovery. This is the message of critical decision theory developed in *Critical Decision Making*, whose application to the selection of technologies, where inflexibilities are particularly obvious, is explored in a general way in *The Social Control of Technology*. *Technology in the Policy Process* extends the discussion, developing an operational meaning for inflexibility using the case of civil nuclear power. Features of technologies are identified which make them inflexible and difficult to control, all of which are found very clearly in atomic power. Respect for error in this way is bound to clash with the belief that getting enough information from science will reduce the risk of mistaken choice to a bearable minimum. What is shown here is that science cannot work like this, that scientists can have no special place in the drama of policymaking, and that our political institutions ought to be structured in recognition of this, by, for example, ensuring a plurality of opinion and a wide spread of political power.

Colin Reeve was supported for this work by a research studentship from the (UK) Joint ESRC/SERC Committee.

Seminars on early versions of the work from which much was learned were given at Aston University, Birmingham University, Leeds University, Manchester University, Oxford University extra-mural department, University College London and the 1984 meeting of the British Society for the Philosophy of Science, Warwick University. Particular thanks for very helpful discussions go to Ian Dyer, Mark Earthey, David Edge, Peter James, Nick Maxwell, Helga Nowotny, Jerry Ravetz, Harry Rothman, Fred Steward, Michael Thompson and Geof Walford.

1 Science and Policy— An Unhappy Marriage

If centuries are to be burdened with names, our own may bear the title of the century of science, so recent is the development of science in the form in which it exists today. In some ways, of course, contemporary science is the inheritor of far older traditions of thought and inquiry, echoing the wonderfully freeminded explorations of the ancient Greek philosophers. For all this, however, at the heart of our science lies a ruthless modernity. Enormous resources have been captured by highly trained and professionalized groups, whose efforts are dedicated to the solution of ever narrower disciplinary problems, whose inconceivably vast output reflects the most intense competitive frenzy.

The science of the century of science is, indeed, a far cry from the early stirrings of the Greeks, striving a little better to know their world. Modern science affects its surrounding society in a number of ways. Most immediately, its products are sometimes of the very greatest intellectual beauty, edifying even the dullest layman. There is no question of the value of science here, but other aspects are of less obvious merit, for example when science is used as a model of rational inquiry which must be aped by less happy fields of human endeavour, from sociology and economics, obsessed with their status as sciences, to politics itself. At a practical level, the science of the twentieth century is seen as the essential motor of technology, taking it far beyond the reaches of empirical, random, trial-and-error experimentation which so limited earlier technical progress. Scientific results are also supposed to illuminate the way for policymakers, which includes all of us at one time or another, in one way or another, who would otherwise be faced with overwhelming uncertainties.

Science as an ideal of intellectual inquiry, as provider of technology and handmaiden to policy has so captured contemporary thinking that it is hard for critical eyes to remain unclouded, the merest hint of doubt about the power of our great servant being greeted with outrage. But for this very reason, criticism of conventional thinking is needed. Work on such a canvas is necessarily piecemeal, this book therefore aims to examine the role of science in the making of policy. It will be necessary to unpick two closely interwoven myths which together support the belief that science can have an important role in political decision-making, the myths of rationality and of the power of science. The first of these myths holds that the first step in making any decision is to reduce the uncertainties with which it is surrounded by gathering in as much relevant information as possible. Occasionally the uncertainties will disappear altogether when this is done, leaving a particularly straightforward decision to be made. But more often there will be a remaining cloud of uncertainty with which the decision-maker must cope as best he may, however it has at least been reduced to the lowest level permitted by existing information. To do otherwise would be to ignore relevant information, a fault which is bound to reduce the chooser's overall benefit from the decision.

Not all of the information required will come from science, of course, some may involve only empirical observation and a little common sense, but as decisions become increasingly complex, the role of science is likely to grow. Here we see how the myth of rationality is woven into the second myth, for it is assumed that science is capable of providing all the information which policy may demand of it. The myth of the power of science holds that whatever information is needed to reduce uncertainty in making a particular policy choice, science can meet the challenge, that the direction of research in science can be quickly and easily changed to provide the information required by policymakers without introducing intolerable delays in the policy process.

The two myths are not empty slogans, for they affect the way policy is conducted. Concern for the social effects of new technology led the United States Congress to establish the Office of Technology Assessment in 1972, charged with the provision and analysis of information on these problems to Congress and the wider public. It is very telling to see how the new agency interpreted its task, which it saw as gathering together information on all aspects of a proposed new technology—social, economic, environmental and political—and not simply the immediate short-term consequences, but the longer-term, remote consequences as well. Since then, of course, experience has chastened the great optimism of the early days of technology assessment, but the total overview is still represented as the aim to which analysis ought to be addressed, even though some compromise with harsh reality has always to be made. The same belief in the powers of information and of science is seen in the American procedures under the Natural Environment Protection Act (NEPA) which calls for detailed and fully researched environmental impact statements to be made about any major project which might harm the environment. Again, the belief is that the benefits of projects can only be balanced against their environmental costs when the latter can be seen in complete detail, established through scientific research. The production of vast, almost entirely unread environmental impact statements is now quite a cottage industry in America, even a modest report occupying several thousand pages giving work to scores of scientists.

Love of data and a belief in science are not a purely North American affair. The British Windscale inquiry of 1977, for example, concerning the building of a reprocessing plant for spent nuclear fuel in Cumbria, is a monument to the myth of rationality, since the public inquiry was forced by political opposition to nuclear power to consider not just the plant proposed, but all aspects of nuclear policy. Information on the plant's safety, costs and environmental problems was gathered, together with the need for nuclear power plants, conservation, alternative energy sources, energy forecasting, and so on and so on. A repeat performance of the whole exercise is at present under way concerning the proposal to build a pressurized water reactor at Sizewell in Suffolk, which has taken even longer and has generated an even greater mileage of reports. Similar debates on nuclear power have taken even longer in Austria, the Netherlands and Sweden. Since much of the information of central importance in these decisions is scientific, these reports serve to entrench the second myth—of the power of science to assist policy.

Technical devices which are presented as aids to policy-making, such as cost-benefit analysis and energy modelling, also serve the twin myths by demanding a great deal of information before they can be applied to a particular policy issue, much of which is to be provided by scientific research. As well as the examples already mentioned, scientific research on an impressive scale in the hope of serving policy is under way on the environmental problems of lead, acid rain, ozone, the greenhouse effect, asbestos, the nuclear winter, pesticides of various sorts, agricultural fertilizers, animal fat, and so on and so on, remembering that each entry on the list really covers a number of research programmes. Although they may hide behind avowals of neutrality and disinterestedness, pretending to be mere providers of information, the simple truth is that the greater the concern of scientific experts in policymaking, the less room there is for ordinary mortals to influence the decisions which affect them. In Nowotny's words (1982, p. 109):

In today's scientized world it would be hard to imagine getting along without experts. The widespread belief in scientific rationality has invaded all features of modern life: problems are primarily defined in ways that suggest scientific and technological solutions and experts are looked upon as the problem solvers. . . . the problem-class, in which expert assessment and recommendations are in demand, has grown as well as the uses to which expertise is put.

After presenting a study of the Austrian debate over nuclear power, she concludes that (p. 123):

vast areas of modern life—technology development and the research process—have virtually been inaccessible and closed to public scrutiny and a modicum of control. Science as a form of cultural domination, with technology as its material incarnation . . . has yet to come to terms with . . . demands for democratization which sound utterly alien to any elite, including the scientific.

The aim of this book is to destroy the twin myths of rationality and of powerful science, replacing them by an account of policymaking which is tailored to the limitations of the human intellect to analyse data, and of science to provide information in a form usable to decision-makers. The myth of rationality is profoundly mistaken; good choices may well be made without first accumulating wagonloads of information in the hope of reducing uncertainty. Indeed, collecting information may actually worsen the quality of decision-making, as noted by the critics of technology assessment, environmental impact statements and of the use of technical devices like cost benefit analysis and energy modelling. Decision-making machinery has been evolved specifically to be able to deal with the inevitable shortfall of information from that demanded by the upholders of the myth of rationality. It is simply not the case that a good decision can only be made once the uncertainties surrounding it have been reduced by gathering as much relevant information as possible. On the contrary, policy decisions may be made quite happily with the very scantiest information.

The myth of the power of science will likewise be rejected. Far from being the natural handmaiden of policy, science is prevented from exerting anything but the most marginal influence over decisions of policy. The conditions for effective scientific research, including the analysis of already existing evidence, cannot be met when the results of science are supposed relevant to policy. Contrary to the myth of the power of science, there is a fundamental and profound mismatch between the needs of policy and the requirements for efficient research within science which forbids science any real influence on decision-making. Such scepticism would be alarming if the first myth, of rationality, were retained, for the impossibility of using science in policymaking would then condemn us all to always make very poor decisions, being unable to reduce the uncertainties involved. But if both myths are rejected at the same time, there is no such problem. If there are perfectly good ways of making policy which do not require the gathering of all relevant information, then it hardly matters that the nature of science prevents us from making such a harvest.

An outline of the book's arguments may now be given. Chapter 2 considers some of the views about the operation of science which sustain the myth of its power to inform the policy process, particularly the belief that properly conducted scientific research yields the truth. If this were indeed the case, the relevance of science to policy would be beyond question, for knowing the truth can hardly hinder decision-making. This belief, and a few like it, are rejected in Chapter 3, in the light of existing views taken of the enterprise of science by the philosophy and sociology of science, and by social studies of science. Contemporary views of science are shown to be an embarrassment for any attempt to defend the traditional thesis that the results of science can be relevant to policy. Scepticism is advanced a little further in Chapter 4 with the articulation of what will be called the over-critical model of expert advice in policymaking. Three conditions for efficient science—autonomy, disciplinarity and a low level of criticism towards conjectures—are shown to be irreparably broken when science tries to assist decision-making. Instead of a consensus being achieved among the scientists which is sufficiently robust to be accepted by all parties to the policy debate, so limiting the area of political disagreement, the political argument feeds a technical dispute which has the potential to continue indefinitely. Any attempt by science to influence policy, on this model, results in endless technical bickering of no value to policy-makers. In Chapter 5 the sceptical thesis of the over-critical model is then tested against a well-known example where scientific research has attempted to influence policy—the control of lead in the environment—which is shown to fit the model. Attempts by scientists to achieve consensus around technical claims which might be relevant to policymaking have, in this case, all failed, and failed for the very reasons identified in the over-critical model.

The emphasis then turns more towards policy, for the operation of the over-critical model in the case of lead raises as an urgent question how policy is to be conducted in this area, given the failure of scientific research to limit the political debate. Chapter 6 therefore looks at the myth of rationality in more detail, showing that policy about the control of environmental lead could never have been made in the way prescribed by the myth's defenders: it would have been impossibly demanding of money, brainpower, time and scientific resources. The following chapter then gives a positive account of policymaking, where choices can be made in an intelligent way without using any significant scientific results, employing the kind of incrementalism championed by Lindblom, showing in particular how policy on lead was made in this way. The remainder of the book consists of more case studies, by which the over-critical model is further tested and articulated.

2 Myths of Science

Myths of two kinds are interwoven in traditional thinking about the relationship between science and policy: the myth of rationality demands that political decisions be made only when all relevant facts have been gathered, that of the power of science insists that science can fulfil this role. A fruitful marriage is therefore promised between knowledge and power. Later chapters built around the case study on policy-making about lead in the environment will pay particular attention to the myth of rational political choice and present more realistic alternatives; for the present our concern is centred more on science. Various aspects of the myth of powerful science will be discussed in the present chapter, and discarded in the next where a more modest conception of the abilities of science will be defined, in keeping with contemporary views of the scientific activity.

'Revolutionary' would not be an understatement for the changes which have occurred since 1945 in our conception of science, yet one corner of human activity seems to have escaped any but the smallest disturbance during these turbulent decades. Conventional views of the usefulness of science for policymaking have resisted significant changes despite the dramatic changes which have occurred in thinking about the methods and practices of science. The aim of this book is at last to remedy this schizophrenia, consigning conventional accounts of science in policymaking to the intellectual dustbin where they have belonged for so long, and developing a new account which is wholly consistent with contemporary thought about the workings and status of science and its products. The myth of the power of science is itself composed of many subsidiary myths, the most important of which will be described in the rest of the chapter.

Science Yields the Truth

Our central question is the power of scientific research to aid the making of political choices, for example about recent policy issues such as acid rain, lead in petrol, the nuclear winter, and so on. Can the research efforts of scientists be quickly and easily directed to finding answers for the urgent factual questions which arise in formulating policy in such areas? In happier times, the question was hardly worth explicit attention, for science was seen as the natural handmaiden of policy. Whatever the shocks and vicissitudes inherent in policymaking, the results of science, the fruits of applying scientific method, could be depended on absolutely, for they are known to be true, or at least known to possess a very high probability. Science provides the truth about the world in which we must co-operate with our fellows in making policy decisions; what it tells us is therefore crucial to how we go about reaching our objectives or compromising with others engaged in the same pursuit. Objectives without factual knowledge have no consequences for action. Nothing follows from the aim of prolonging human life until scientific research reveals facts, for example that diets high in animal fats cause premature death, whereupon policy directed towards limiting such eating habits can be pursued. Dissent can be expected, farmers may try to resist these policies, but this can only be a reflection of the different relative values accorded to additional years of life and wealthy farmers, for even the farmers must accept the deliverance of qualified scientific experts about the consequences of the eating habits they have investigated.

Although such an elevated view of science belongs to the history books, its influence lives on in the belief that science can be highly relevant to practical matters of policy. It often happens that views live on past their time, hardly changing long after the theoretical ideas which once underpinned them have become jokes of the seminar room. The thesis that scientific method leads to the truth, or at least to statements of high probability, has virtually no contemporary adherents in the philosophy, the sociology and the social studies of science. Where the older view regarded the empirical evidence provided by experiment as the bedrock which had to be accepted by all scientists as they developed theories about the workings of the world, contemporary accounts of science, which will be discussed in more detail in the following chapter, stress the room for manoeuvre which always exists in the acceptance of any scientific claim, including ones about what has been observed. For Popper, science is a continual process of conjecture and refutation, hypothesis and criticism. The claims of science cannot be known to be true, nor known to have a high probability; they are, instead, guesses about the world, which may in turn be criticized by other guesses. Kuhn presents science as a superbly efficient problem-solving machine. As for Popper, the rationality of science lies not in its power to once and for all uncover truth, but in its ability to resolve local anomalies very effectively. Sociologists of science have recently stressed the provisional nature of all scientific consensus, for agreement is not forced on the scientists by their observations of the world; it is, like all agreements, a product of social interaction, negotiations within the implicitly accepted rules of the game of science. Agreement is sometimes fragile, however, and can break down under social stresses with the reopening of a whole number of views originally regarded as closed.

Whatever the differences between these views of science, they have in common an emphasis on the tentative nature of scientific claims, the possibility of many interpretations of any body of experimental results, the overthrow of one idea for another. On such views of science, its usefulness for policymaking is obviously open to doubt, and yet little has been done to explore this sceptical avenue. If the conjectures which today's scientists accept are bound to be rejected sooner or later, just as the conjectures which seemed so compelling yesterday have been given up, of what use can they be in offering guidance to policymakers?

Experts can be Expected to Agree

Since science discovers the truth, its practitioners can be expected to agree about the facts. Consensus is the normal state of science, debate and disagreement marking, at best, an inadvertent failure to apply scientific method properly, or, at worst, outright bias and distortion by one of the parties. If the experts have correctly followed the rules of scientific method and have considered all the available data, then they ought to reach the same conclusion. This view is particularly attractive to policymakers who obviously hope for a consensus from among their scientific advisers; dissent merely adds to the policymakers' problems as they become even less sure about how to achieve their objectives.

Two immediate consequences of great importance follow from the expectation of consensus among scientists. Policy debates must be based upon differences in the values of each side, since they must agree about the facts of the matter, whatever experts they may have consulted. Disagreements about action which continue beyond the point where confusions and misunderstandings about the facts have been cleared up, must reflect the different values with which each side operates, as in the example of the farmers who objected to policy directed against high-fat diets discussed earlier. The second consequence is that there is a problem about the disagreements which experts occasionally have. How are these to be explained? If disagreement of this sort survives the surveying of the relevant facts, it can only reveal the operation of bias in one of the disputants. Bias receives a psychological characterization, being a distortion produced by some vested interest in drawing conclusions from the available data, or in deciding just what data is available. Bias may be avoided by ensuring that scientific experts advising policymakers have no interests in the outcome of the policy, one way or another.

Scientists who are disinterested in the outcome of policy, and who may therefore be employed as advisers, will have no political role in the making of policy, their task being only to provide information for decision-makers to use in whatever way they may want. What Habermas (1971) calls the 'decisionistic model' and Clark (1974) the 'democratic paradigm' are descriptions of this barrier between the providers of scientific knowledge and the political consumers of scientific knowledge. Warnings about the maintenance of the barrier are common. Laski (1931) urges that expert advisers should have no greater influence on policy than any other citizens, and US Secretary of Defence, Harold Brown (1977), has warned against advocacy by experts.

If in the guise of analysis and exposition, an expert becomes an advocate for a particular decision, he sometimes may have his own way, but only by substituting his own judgement for that of people who have the responsibility for decisions and who might weigh values differently if given all the facts, and whose judgement may be better.

Similar remarks are from Phillip Handler (1975), speaking as President of the US National Academy of Sciences: 'science can study whether energy independence is technically possible or whether Soviet underground nuclear tests can be detected, but must then let regular policymakers decide whether to try for energy independence or just what arms control proposals to put to the Russians.'

Russell (1982) points out that the barrier between politicians making policy and their scientific advisers is supposed to be found in risk assessment—the scientists assessing the objective magnitude of the risk, the policymakers then deciding on whether it is acceptable, though in reality the picture is far from the pretended ideal. Hadden (1977), surveying several aspects of policymaking, found widespread belief in the democratic paradigm among American policymakers.

Science is One

A further consequence of seeing science as a vehicle for delivering the truth, or a set of highly probable claims, is that science must be seen as essentially a unity, something particularly stressed by twentieth-century empiricists. The methods employed in arriving at the truth may vary between scientific disciplines—the ways of organic chemistry are not quite the ways of paleobotany—but by whatever route they arrive at the truth, their common terminus gives the disciplines far more in common than any details of operational procedure may separate them. Whether or not a practitioner from one discipline can fully understand the work of someone in another discipline, there should be a natural state of trust across disciplinary divides. Provided there is a consensus within a discipline that a claim is true, it must be accepted as such by scientists in any other discipline, just as it must by laymen. Organic chemists may find the work of paleobotanists fairly hard reading, but for all that they must accept the consensus among paleobotanists as much as they insist paleobotanists respect whatever agreement is reached within organic chemistry. There ought not to be any major barriers of communication between workers in different disciplines—a point of particular relevance to policy problems which invariably require scientific research in a number of disciplines. We shall see later that this is entirely false.

The Principle of Irrelevance

What will be termed the principle of irrelevance states that the assessment of a scientific idea should not in any way be influenced by the use to which it might eventually be put. The truth discovered by scientists is the truth and remains so whatever implications it may have for policy. Truth shall speak though the heavens fall; if the rose of truth be thorned, then we shall bleed. On the surface, the principle of irrelevance may appear to be an obvious condition for any rational enterprise; however, good reasons will later be given for its rejection. The principle is a consequence of the view that science yields the truth, and indeed the principle will be seen to fall with this view. The aim of policy is to use the facts revealed by science to further some objective, and the facts can hardly be allowed to change as the aims of policy alter. Changes in policy can make people regret what the facts are, but they are beyond revision. Policy objectives will obviously influence the research topics undertaken by scientists, but the methods employed in that research should be the same as in research which is remote from policy, and its results will likewise be independent of any use that might be made of them. We shall see later how this too is a mistaken view, the deepest workings of science are irresistibly altered when science becomes involved in policy.

The principle of irrelevance is closely related to the myth of the impenetrable barrier between scientist, as factual adviser, and those who use these facts for making policies, as recognized by Elwood and Gallacher (1984).

science and social policy have asymmetric relations. Social policy determines which hypotheses are sufficiently important to be tested but cannot legitimately influence the interpretation of the data in terms of predictive relations. Science, on the other hand, can serve only to predict and cannot legitimately interpret the social importance of the predictions . . . the two processes are quite distinct and must be conducted exclusively on their own terms. If these distinctions are not observed, both science and social policy will suffer, the contribution of science will become less trustworthy and the outcome of policy less secure.

Policy can be Based on Science

Science, revealing as it does the truth, can be relied upon with confidence in the process of policymaking. Knowing the truth, policymakers can decide how best to fulfil their objectives and can plot a course of action which has a very high probability of achieving maximum returns. Policy, in other words, is very sensitive to the results of science: science plays a very important role in the determination of policy. It will be very useful to quantify this idea of the confidence which policymakers place in the results given to them by their scientific advisers, which may be done through the idea of error cost—a key concept throughout the present work. Consider a technological example first. Imagine a pharmaceutical firm which is advised by its pharmacologists that a new product is a safe cure for a particular ailment. The firm's board must choose from a number of options: at one extreme the construction of a new plant at a cost of £10 million, at the other continued research in the laboratory at a modest level. The cost of the pharmacologists' advice being wrong—the error cost—is, in the first case, £10 million (at least) and in the second, just a few thousand pounds per year. If the firm decides to build the plant, then it places great confidence in the advice and the decision may be said to be highly sensitive to that advice. If the pharmacologists' conjecture was not accepted, the firm would never build such a plant. At the other extreme, if the favoured option is to continue bench research, the company places a low degree of confidence in the conjecture of its pharmacologists and its choice is insensitive to that conjecture. This laboratory research might well be valuable even though the conjecture is false. This suggests that error cost may be used as a measure of the sensitivity of a conjecture in making a decision.

To generalize, imagine a decision-maker informed of conjecture F which makes him alter his preferred options from A to B. If F is false, the decision-maker has erred, for A would still be the favoured option. The cost of this mistake, of choosing B instead of A when F is false, is the error cost. A low error cost implies a low sensitivity of the choice to the conjecture F. This is easily seen for in the limiting case A and B are identical and the decision-maker's option is completely uninfluenced by F. Even if the decision-maker knew that F was false, he would not change his option, making the error cost zero. Clearly, in this case the sensitivity of the choice to F is also zero. On the other hand, B may be a radically different course of action from A, one which would never have been adopted but for F. In this case the error cost is large, as is the sensitivity of the choice to F. In short, the degree of influence of a scientific conjecture on a decision may be measured by error cost. The optimism of the conventional view of the relationship between science and policy may now be expressed by saying that it supposes that policy can be sensitive to the results of scientific research, that policies may be based upon the findings of science even where these have a high error cost.

In this chapter we have considered in outline some of the myths which congregate under the umbrella myth of the power of science and which make great promises for the ability of science to inform politics. It is time to develop a more realistic, and an altogether more humble, view of science and its importance for policy, which is the task of the next chapter.

3 Realities of Science

Modern conceptions of science forged by philosophers and sociologists of science and workers in the social studies of science could not be more different from the earlier views of the subject discussed briefly in the previous chapter. There is much argument about the details of this conception, but the outlines have been clear enough for all to see for many years.

Science does not Yield the Truth

The principle underpinning the earlier elevation of science, that its methods reveal the truth, has been dismissed as an impossibility. Popper (1959) sees science, not as delivering the truth, but as consisting of guesses which are subject to test against other guesses. Scientific method is a set of rules ensuring that the conjectures of science are open to criticism and the possibility of rejection. Criticism is only possible if rival theories are encouraged, attention therefore being focused on the room which always exists for rival interpretations of any body of data. Whatever consensus may exist among scientists is always likely to be broken at any moment by the discovery of some new phenomenon or simply by a change in scientific fashion. In contrast to earlier views of science, observations are not able to force scientists into agreement, indeed, statements about experimental results are as open to error as any other claim within science. While recognizing that all scientific claims should be open to criticism, it is realized that too much criticism would easily destroy the whole enterprise of science. Limits must therefore be placed on the extent of criticism, a point which will later prove to be of very great importance for our understanding of the role which science may play in policymaking. Kuhn (1970) agrees with many of these points, although he describes the workings of science without reference to truth. Empirical results are always open to more than one interpretation, and consensus may be short-lived.

Mulkay (1979) tells the story of the growing confidence of

sociologists in analysing the contents of science. If the theories held by scientists are determined by their observations, as with traditional accounts of science, there is no scope for asking for any explanations as to why these theories were chosen. Once it becomes clear, however, that many rival interpretations of evidence are always open, it is possible to look for the social factors influencing the selection, a point of great importance in understanding conflicts which arise when the interpretations which are offered are of relevance to some question of policy. As for truth, many sociologists adopt a robust relativism, since it is a non-operational concept, unlike belief or commitment or consensus.

Experts can be Expected to Disagree

On earlier views of science, disputes between experts could only be seen as an aberration caused by bias from some vested interest, but on contemporary views there is always the possibility of disagreement about what interpretation some body of evidence ought to receive. There is now room for debates about policy to be something other than the head-on clash of values allowed by earlier conceptions of science which held that its results had to be accepted by everyone. Policy debates may now be about what interpretation should be given to scientific findings. In this way, disagreement among experts is not at all shocking: it is a sign of a healthy policy process where rival views are pitched one against another. In an example to be discussed later in some depth, those concerned to protect the environment, including the United States Environmental Protection Agency (EPA) have interpreted the libraries of research findings relevant to the matter as showing that lead from motor vehicles damages the health of young children. The industry, however, is able to articulate and defend the contrary interpretation, that lead from its products is not harmful to children, despite the quantity of the evidence over which the dispute ranges. This would not be allowed on earlier views of science, which would have to hold one side as biased in its refusal to accept the evident truth attested to by scientific method.

Collingridge (1982, 1984b) has analysed some examples of

such disputes and a great many empirical studies of expert disagreement have revealed the importance of this kind of
dispute over the interpretation of data, for example Clark
(1974), Doty (1972), Fallows (1979), Gillespie *et al.* (1979),
Hadden (1979), Holcomb (1970), Knopp (1979), Mazur
(1973), Nelkin (1971), Nowotny and Hirsch (1980), Peterson
and Markle (1979), Priebe and Kaufman (1980), Reiser
(1966), Robbins and Johnston (1976). In her introduction to a
collection of case studies, Nelkin (1979, p. 16) observes that
'whatever political values motivate controversy, the debates
usually focus on technical questions'. Experts occasionally
agree on technical matters which are relevant to policy, but
this is a rare event which cannot be taken as a model for the
correct relationship between science and policy. Technical
debates between rival groups of experts over the interpretation of data are concerned exclusively with facts, and
explicit mention of values are generally rare, although, of
course, it is often a deep difference in values and interests
which motivates actors in the policy process to articulate a
technical case. Thus, the lead industry defended a technical
case which protected its profit, and the Environmental Protection Agency's technical case served the organization's need to
show off its power as a new star in the bureaucratic heavens,
although neither the industry's profit nor the Agency's political needs received any explicit mention in the debate between
them.

This has profound consequences for the view taken of the
scientists' role in policymaking and the nature of bias within
the process of decision-making. The only way to ensure a
genuine healthy debate between rival groups of experts is to
motivate them to scrutinize their opponents' views critically,
and to develop their own case as the argument continues and
as new research results are added to the stock already under
discussion. Scientists, to be effective, ought to be interested
parties, not the neutral, disinterested, detached observers of
mythology. They act, in the words of Collingridge (1980),
more like advocates in a court of law than neutral scientists in
the laboratory. There are good common-sense reasons which
force us to recognize this point, quite apart from considerations of theories about the workings of science. In forming an

opinion relevant to policy, a scientist must do much more than the customary evaluation of each scientific paper which passes across his bench. What is needed is a review of existing literature to see whether a technical case can be made out that, for example, lead from petrol damages children, that sulphur dioxide affects tree growth, or whatever the issue may be. A good advocate will scrutinize the available evidence intently, searching thoroughly for items which can be fitted into the jigsaw of such a case, and the estimation of each piece of the puzzle will inevitably be affected by whether or not it fits with the pieces already assembled. If the case is sick and lame, this may be discovered by criticism from opposing advocates, but at least the technical case has been assembled around which debate can be organized in an intelligent way. The second point is that a scientific result is no more than ink on paper until it is brought to the attention of actors within the policy-making process. Where a disinterested researcher would note the point, an effective advocate will bring it to the attention of those to whom it might be of value, forcing down the well-known barriers which all policymakers have to build for self-protection against being inundated with information.

Bias exists in the process of policymaking where freedom to challenge interpretations placed on data by others is impossible, for whatever reason. As Collingridge (1980) points out, bias characterized in this way is not a psychological feature of experts, but an objectively identifiable and hence remediable feature of the way policy is being made, examples of which will be given later. Bias of this sort might be, for example, the impossibility of challenging various claims made by experts because of the law governing public inquiries, or the domination of one field of research by a narrow group of experts who cannot be effectively challenged since they control the funding of research and the publication outlets.

Enough has been said to show that scientific advisers are not the simple providers of information which the democratic paradigm, itself supported by the myths of science described earlier, insists upon. The barrier between technical adviser and political actor can no longer be maintained. As an advocate, the scientist must search for a case to please his master and fight to ensure that whatever results fit that case are brought to the attention of his paymaster. Nowotny (1984) discusses the problem scientists have in reconciling serving such a function with the more traditional ethos which they have inherited.

Science is Many

The modern view of science paints a much richer picture of the various disciplines which seem essential for its successful operation than earlier empiricist conceptions of science. Disciplines are now seen as essential to the workings of science rather than as a fine point of its social organization. Kuhn (1970) is particularly valuable here. Science, for Kuhn, is necessarily divided into a very large number of disciplines, each operating with its own particular and defining paradigm which is shared by all the discipline's practitioners. The most important part of the paradigm are its exemplars, a set of standard problems and solutions against which all other scientific work is to be judged. Initiates of the discipline are taught these exemplars not as factual matters, but as guides to understanding the world; they are taught to see all other problems in the same way and to search for solutions which are the same as those of the standard solutions. This agreement, achieved by education and enshrined in text books, ensures that researchers in the discipline can focus their efforts into technical puzzles of the most refined narrowness, in the process of what Kuhn calls 'normal science'. There is a clear understanding of what puzzles exist and although they are not yet solved, what their solution would look like is recognized. Communication between workers in the same discipline is therefore extraordinarily easy since all the fundamentals are agreed upon: what is a problem, what is a solution, what standards of accuracy are appropriate, what techniques may and may not be used, what journals and text books are worth reading and what can safely be left on the shelf, and so on. Many puzzles will be too easy to merit the effort of researchers and others will be too hard to be worth tackling, but the distribution of rewards to researchers in the discipline, by way of publications, employment, praise and prizes, ensures that research concentrates on puzzles with an optimum trade-off between importance and solubility. In Kuhn's (1970, p. 144) words, 'In its normal state . . . a scientific community is an immensely efficient instrument for solving the problems or puzzles that its paradigms define'.

But efficient communication within a discipline can only be achieved at the cost of very poor communications across scientific disciplines. This can only really be achieved by a scientist being fully trained, from the beginning, in two or more disciplines. Anything short of this, and communication becomes bedevilled by misunderstandings and confusion owing to the operation of the different rules which have been internalized by the workers in the different disciplines. Many ideas and experimental procedures and standards will be quite different, and even greater confusion is generated by the existence of an apparently shared vocabulary which actually receives subtly different interpretations within the disciplines.

Similar conclusions are reached by other researchers, mostly in the sociology of science, who stress the operation of tacit knowledge, unwritten rules of conduct and craft skills in the functioning of scientific disciplines, for example Collins (1981), Harvey (1981), Pickering (1981, 1984), Pinch (1981), Travis (1981), Ravetz (1973). An important study here is that of Collins (1975) which analysed the arguments within physics over the detection of gravity waves. Collins concentrated on the process by which scientists decide whether an experiment is a replication of an earlier one or a wholly new experiment. The algorithmic model, according to which there is a finite series of unambiguous instructions which can be formulated for the operation of an experiment which can therefore be used to produce a copy of an earlier experiment is quickly rejected. In its place, Collins suggests an enculturation model where the question of replication is settled, not by following a rule book, but by negotiation with fellow scientists in the disciplines involved. If the apparatus yields different results from previous experiments, this by itself cannot establish that the two experiments are different, for they could be the same experiment, the difference in performance resulting from poor observation or careless manipulation of the ironware. Negotiation towards a consensus is required even on such fundamental questions about the replication or otherwise of an experiment. This underlines the problems of communication across disciplines which Kuhn describes. Rule books would enable any competent experimentalist from one discipline to conduct useful experiments in another discipline, but their absence means that an outsider must enter into negotiations with insiders, negotiations which involve all kinds of implicit assumptions, tacit knowledge and craft skills peculiar to the discipline. The outsider's only hope for effective communication and for doing significant research in the new discipline is to completely retrain, going through the same enculturation processes shared by those he wishes to join. Anything less than this inevitably leads to defective communication and hence to research of poor quality.

Research in the social studies of science on the use which is made of scientific results in policymaking underlines the problems which research in several disciplines generates. Robbins and Johnston (1976), for example, studied the conflict between a number of prominent industrial hygienists and the geochemist Patterson over the health effects of lead found in the normal environment. At this time, much of the research on lead concerned industrial exposure and was dominated by a group of professional industrial hygienists. Central to their view of lead poisoning is the belief that there is some threshold below which everyone is sure of being safe. The problem for the industry is then to ensure that none of its workers cross the threshold, which on the basis of accumulated experience was put at a blood level of 80 μg/100 ml. Workers whose blood showed greater concentrations of the metal were screened out and given treatment or shifted to a job less exposed to lead. The existence of the threshold greatly simplifies the work of the hygienists, but for all that there is no reason to suppose that it was not a scientifically respectable position. Work by hygienists on environments remote from industry had revealed very similar levels of lead to those found in industrial areas, the conclusion being that most of this material must have come from rocks and not from industrial pollution. Early man therefore developed in an environment with quite high levels of lead and is therefore likely to have

inherited an immunity to it. Only industrial workers are therefore at risk from the metal.

Patterson shook the cosy consensus of the hygienists, arguing that lead levels in remote areas had been hugely exaggerated through contamination of specimens. If proper care
were taken to ensure cleanliness, lead levels in such places
were barely detectable. This caused the most violent reaction
from the hygienists through their journal and through other
publications, who questioned the competence of Patterson to
express any judgement about lead, and the right of geochem-
istry to invade their own territory. Robbins and Johnston see
the heat as generated not by a simple factual disagreement, but
by Patterson's questioning of the threshold concept so central
to the discipline of industrial hygiene, and the implied challenge to the occupational niche enjoyed by hygienists in the
lead industry.

Surveying work in all these fields, it is clear that the happy
picture of cross-disciplinary communication painted by the
traditional empiricist accounts of science changes very radically when a more realistic view of science is taken. Science is
not one but many; it is riven by disciplinary divides which are
essential for its proper working but confound attempts at
cross-disciplinary research. The problem is, of course, that
there is no reason to think that the factual issues demanding an
urgent solution for policymakers will fall neatly into the
disciplinary boxes which scientists have drawn up for their
work.

The Principle of Relevance

The principle of irrelevance, stating that the assessment of a
scientific conjecture should be independent of any use to
which the conjecture may be put, seems innocent enough at
first, but on further analysis it must go, indeed it must be
replaced by its converse, the principle of relevance, which
holds that the uses to which any scientific conjecture is to be
put shall always influence its assessment. This sounds quite
shocking when assessment is taken as discovering whether the
conjecture is true or false, but we have seen that this is an

empty dream of empiricism. Conjectures cannot be established as true; at the most they may be criticized as conflicting with other conjectures which are held. A whole new dimension to methodology is introduced at this point, for criticism may be applied across a wide spectrum of intensity. A conjecture in science may be subjected to anything from the most intense criticism, or to practically none at all.

Philosophers and sociologists of science have faced up to the problem in a number of ways. Popper insists that critical enthusiasm must be tempered by dogmatism if science is to have any hope of making progress, for there is unlimited room for critical attack. Popper (1969) therefore proposes the rule that a conjecture should be rejected only if it can be replaced by a rival conjecture which has excess corroborated content, banning the purely negative search for as many flaws as possible in a given theory. Building on this suggestion, Lakatos (1970) developed the idea of research programmes, whose core conjectures are supposed to be immune from falsification which is always turned towards the outer protective belt of hypotheses. In this way, the theories of the core are saved from premature rejection, their worth only becoming apparent after some time. Kuhn's paradigms serve the same purpose, for criticism of fundamentals is no longer allowed—an essential step if normal science is to enable researchers to concentrate on ever more minute problems. Restriction of criticism in this way marks the end of the chaos of pre-scientific research and the start of a vastly more efficient puzzle-solving engine. Sociologists of science such as Harvey (1981) have restated the problem as being how debates may be closed, recognizing that any argument, for example about the truth of a particular theory, has the potential to last forever. There is no external force to coerce one side into agreement with the other; in particular, observations can be doubted and interpreted differently. Science can only progress with tacit rules which limit debate, enabling argument to close around a consensus, at least for the time being.

This is not the place to survey all the suggestions of this kind which have been made. For present purposes it is more important to recognize the universally accepted problem of limiting criticism within science, for science becomes impossible if it is given free rein. A flourishing science demands a low level of criticism, or to put it differently, a high level of conjecture. Under this regime, conjecture and specu- lation flourish, many rival ideas being entertained at any one time. The premature rejection of a conjecture is seen as worse than holding on to a discredited idea for a little too long.

There is an intimate connection between the level of criticism which is appropriate for a conjecture and the error cost associated with the conjecture. On listening to a radio report of the latest conjectures about the effects of gases from aerosol cans on the upper atmosphere, a man might change his method of shaving, reverting from aerosol can to the more primitive soap and water. If the conjecture is false, if gases from these cans do not, after all, pollute the atmosphere, then the decision to change to soap and water is also mistaken, the error cost being the extra economic cost of shaving and any additional discomfort and injury. If an aircraft is built along lines suggested by a new theory of aerodynamics, which happens to be false, so that the plane flies like a lead duck, then the error cost is the expense of development plus the pain and frustration associated with the fiasco. If the use of a scientific conjecture has a high error cost, it makes sense to search for errors very vigorously; it is rational to subject a conjecture to severe criticism when the cost of it being false is high. In decid- ing how critical to be towards a scientific conjecture, what else can be appealed to except the costs which error would impose? For conjectures whose use has a low error cost, it is perfectly in order to act upon the conjecture without spending much effort in criticism; a low degree of criticism is appro- priate where the cost of a mistake is low. The cost of changing one's shaving method is likely to be so trivial as to be worth doing on the merest hint that aerosol gases interfere with the earth's atmosphere. It is certainly quite inappropriate to spend years of research effort in atmospheric chemistry before being sure enough about the deleterious effects of aerosols to change one's customary morning routine. Quite otherwise, however, in the case of the plane. If success for a multi-million development programme crucially depends on a particular theory of aerodynamics, it is advisable to spend time and effort testing the conjecture. In short, the level of criticism appropriate to a scientific conjecture is determined, at least in part, by the costs which would arise from using a mistaken conjecture. Adjusting the level of criticism to the use to which the conjecture will be put breaches the principle of irrelevance. But this should not be alarming: the principle has no role to play in a modern conception of scientific method. It must be rejected along with the hope that science yields the truth. If the essence of scientific method is criticism, then it is intelligent to look for errors more searchingly when mistakes will be expensive. To adopt a uniform level of criticism in obedience to the principle of irrelevance would be grotesquely irrational.

The low level of criticism customary in pure science can now be explained as a reflection of the low error cost associated with its conjectures. Reputations may be a little bruised, to be sure, but what does it really matter if a group of pure scientists hold beliefs which happen to be false—opinions which will never be acted upon beyond the laboratory and lecture room? The picture is very different when science is involved in practical affairs of policy where the cost of error may not infrequently include the health and even the lives of millions of people, many of them perhaps unborn. A much more vigorous search for error is appropriate here than is ever needed in pure science. In practical affairs, scientists themselves, and those wishing to use their results, therefore become much more critical towards findings which threaten their deep interests. It must be stressed that the rise in the temperature of criticism when science leaves the laboratory is a perfectly rational feature of debate and policymaking. It is not that the parties are besmirching the purity of scientific method because of their need to protect their interests; they are, on the contrary, exercising their right to be very critical of ideas which have a high error cost for them. Just because scientists agree that a particular conjecture is the best one to accept for further testing and theoretical elaboration, it can hardly mean that this guess is the one to be acted upon in matters of life and death.

So influential are the myths of science discussed earlier, including the principle of irrelevance, that the above discussion is bound to cause offence, for which no apology is offered. We may sympathize with the medical epidemiologist

OLSON LIBRARY
NORTHERN MICHIGAN UNIVERSITY
MARQUETTE, MICHIGAN 49855

Bradford Hill (1965), as he struggles under the burden of conventional thinking to make the point of this section:

in passing from association to causation I believe in real life we shall have to consider what flows from that decision. On scientific grounds we should do no such thing. The evidence is there to be judged on its merits and the judgement (in that sense) should be utterly independent of what hangs upon it—or who hangs because of it. But in another and more practical sense we may surely ask what is involved in our decision. In occupational medicine our object is usually to take action. If this be operative cause and that deleterious effect, then we shall wish to intervene to abolish or reduce death or disease.

Policy cannot be Based on Science

The optimism engendered by traditional views of science about the relevance of its theories to policymaking has been questioned in recent years, on the basis of empirical studies of the application of science to particular problems of policy, and more theoretically informed studies of the nature of the policy process. Attention has already been drawn to a number of studies which report how scientific debates about the inter-pretation of data arise when research is seen as relevant to policy, and it is far from clear what influence scientific research can have on the policies which finally emerge in such a situation. It may be, as Nelkin (1971, 1975) suggests from her survey of many case studies, that bands of experts com-mitted to a given policy do their best to provide technical evidence in its support, but then any influence they may have is often cancelled out by a rival group of experts proclaiming evidence for the contrary course of action. Empirical studies of the use of research results to policymakers such as Weiss and Bucuvalas (1980), Weiss (1977) and Caplan *et al.* (1975) reinforce this sceptical conclusion. Ravetz (1973) also points to more general problems indicating a serious mismatch between science and policy—what he calls the 'management of exactness'. Experts are generally expected by their paymasters to provide hard facts expressed in precise numbers, and are not likely to be aware of the inexactitude attending all quantifi-cation. Scientists may therefore disagree about the exactness of specific items of data, particularly probabilistic data, which undermines the usefulness of their results for the making of policy.

Defenders of incrementalism in policymaking, notably Lindblom, have emphasized the problems which policy-makers encounter when trying to base their judgement on the results of science. Four problems arise. Scientific data for use in policy is very expensive to acquire, and moreover delays the whole policy process while being gathered, which may itself be taken as a cost. Delay often means that by the time the scientific results are written up, the policy problem has changed, and the research is no longer relevant, being the answer to yesterday's questions. Policy is notoriously volatile, where science needs time to produce results of any significance. The final problem is that of co-ordinating all the scientific results which are supposed relevant to the policy choices which are open. These points may be treated a little superficially at the moment, for a more extended treatment will come later, in Chapter 7. For these reasons incrementalists favour making piecemeal, *ad hoc* decisions which place very little reliance upon the results of scientific research. Armed with the technical device of error cost, their position may be restated as holding that policy is and ought to be insensitive to any scientific results; whatever hypotheses are used in policy are and ought to be of a low error cost. Hammond *et al.* (1983) discusses many problems in the use of science for policymaking, but the value of their comments is reduced by their uncritical adoption of the rational actor model of decision-making, which will be attacked in Chapter 6.

This chapter has considered some of the recent developments in thinking about science which threaten the traditional myth of the power of science to inform policy. From all sides, this must be abandoned. Chapter 4 will build upon the present discussion by formulating clearly and precisely a hypothesis about the real relationship between science and policy, which can be tested in later chapters.

4 The Over-critical Model

The previous chapters looked at the many myths which have traditionally underpinned the assumption that science is a natural handmaiden to policy. Science is supposed to deliver the truths so urgently needed for making intelligent choices and unanimity can be expected from scientists about the truth. The interdisciplinary nature of the questions posed by policy are glossed over by the belief that science speaks with one voice, that the disciplines within it are little more than an administrative convenience. The principle of irrelevance protects the workings of science from any damaging outside influence: science can be of use to policy without becoming besmirched if the barrier between scientists and the users of their results is maintained. Science is just as powerful whether its results are confined to the academy or applied outside to pressing matters of the moment. Given these stories about the noble enterprise, it is hardly surprising to find such widespread confidence in the power of science to assist policymakers.

But the myths are by now looking very tired and the previous chapter reviewed some of the sources of its fatigue in the philosophy and the sociology of science, social studies of science and political theory. None of the myths supporting the traditional conception of science's special role in policymaking can now be upheld; science does not deliver truth; unanimity among scientists is rare and often unwelcome; science is deeply riven with disciplinary boundaries which create great problems for the sort of interdisciplinary research which policy demands; and there are serious difficulties in matching the needs of policy and research in science. In the light of this discussion, it is not surprising to find that the principal thesis of this book, to be stated in the present chapter, is the sceptical one that no choices of policy are ever made which are sensitive to any scientific conjecture, and that no such choice ought to be sensitive to any scientific hypothesis.

The double statement captures the important point that the

book's thesis is at one and the same time both descriptive of existing practice and prescriptive in that it lays down rules for good policymaking. Twin claims of this sort are customary in discussions of theories of action, which lay down ways in which people ought to act to get what they want and also offer explanations for the apparent success people have in choosing what to do. This success is the result of following, in an in- tuitive and often rough-and-ready way, the prescriptions of the theory which says how people ought to act. Without this doubling of prescription and description, it must appear an enormous accident that people generally get what they want through making active decisions and not waiting patiently for providence. In the present case, the corrigibility of all scientific claims means that policy ought to be insensitive to any conjec- ture of science, otherwise very large error costs may be incurred. If a claim is likely to be in error, whether this is discovered late or discovered early, it is wise not to base actions on it which would be very costly if the claim is false. This is a normative claim, of course, but the thesis may be strengthened by holding that the success which seems to attend policymaking in the real world is partly due to its following the prescription against choices which are sensitive to scientific claims. For a more extended discussion see Collingridge (1980).

So far, the thesis of scepticism is very imprecise; it needs much more elaboration if it is to be tested properly—which it may now receive, armed with the insights of the previous chapter. Attempts to influence policy by scientific research all founder in the same way, which will now be elaborated upon. There are at least three conditions for a healthy, flourishing science: autonomy, disciplinarity and a low level of criticism associated with the low error cost of scientific conjectures. The condition of autonomy has not been discussed until now because there has never been a word of criticism against it; from the earliest days to the present it has been recognized that science works at its most efficient if the problems people work on, the resources devoted to these problems and the rewards given for their solution are in the hands of scientists themselves. The old empiricists believed this, as do Popper and Kuhn. In Polanyi's (1962) words, 'the pursuit of science by independent self-coordinated initiatives assures the most efficient possible organization of scientific progress'.

Autonomy is, of course, reduced when research is directed to questions posed by policymakers outside the scientific arena, producing a loss in the quality of research, for such is the price of knowledge which is useful beyond the laboratory. Questions posed by policy are always interdisciplinary, but we have seen that disciplinarity is necessary for the most efficient operation of science. Attempts to answer the questions asked by policy are therefore bound to be less efficient than the usual attacks on disciplinary puzzles; conflict and confusion will be generated as the tacit rules operating within a well-defined discipline are crossed by similar unwritten rules from other disciplines. We have seen that efficient scientific research demands a low level of criticism, achieved by the low error cost associated with research findings of pure science. Where such results are applied to policy, however, error cost increases enormously. The cost of error in pure science is qualitatively different from error costs when science is applied. How, for example, can the cost of thinking rather too well of a particular speculation within pure science be compared to the pain, anguish, suffering and even death which not infrequently accompany errors in the application of science? The low cost of error in pure science gives scientists there the blessing of time in which opinions can be tested out and changed, unlike most applications of science where delay is expensive. Pure scientists have the enormous advantage over the engineers, doctors, dentists, politicians, policymakers and businessmen who seek to apply the results of science, in that their errors are virtually free. Where error is costly, it is reasonable to search diligently for it, adopting a high level of criticism, and this is exactly what is found when attempts are made to employ science to influence policy. The methodological rules restricting criticism which are essential for the efficiency of pure science are quite inappropriate to the new situation where errors have become hugely more costly. The rules crumble and criticism becomes far more intense than in research in pure science.

The sensitivity of a policy decision to a scientific conjecture may be measured by the conjecture's error cost. If the cost of error is large, then great confidence is being placed on the conjecture's truth, giving it a considerable influence over which policy is selected. A low error cost, conversely, implies that little confidence is placed in the conjecture's truth, and the conjecture has little influence over policy. Here is the root of the ruin of the ambition of science to influence policy. Influence calls for the conjecture to have a high error cost, but high error cost makes appropriate an intense critical scrutiny of the conjecture, in contrast to the demands of efficient research. Scientists and policymakers using their results become very critical of scientific reports which threaten their case, and in turn the technical case they make out is criticized by the other side. The result is that no consensus can be reached which is of use in policymaking. If this were not embarrassment enough, loss of autonomy and disciplinarity mean that the research undertaken is of poor quality, and thus particularly easy to criticize. People in the debate wish to be critical and criticism is especially easy. Technical debate therefore becomes endless. Rather than scientific research serving to limit the political debate, argument over policy generates a matching dispute of a technical kind which can well continue indefinitely. Hopes that argument over policy will be narrowed in the light of technical findings evaporate, indeed the very opposite happens, political dissent deepening as those involved become ever more frustrated by their opponent's stubborn refusal to accept what is seen as an overwhelmingly good scientific case. In the words of Nelkin (1979):

When expertise becomes available to both sides of a controversy, it further polarizes conflict by calling attention to areas of technical ambiguity and to the limited ability to predict and control risks. The very existence of conflicting technical interpretations generates political activity. And the fact that experts disagree more than the substance of their disputes, fires controversy.

The technical debate concerns rival interpretations of the available evidence, and as such refers exclusively to factual claims, although, of course, the explanation for the dispute is generally a deep divide of interests and values. Some of the scientists act as advocates, searching the literature for results which can be put together as a technical case supporting their own interests, or the interests of their paymasters, and fighting off counterclaims as effectively as possible. There may, of course, be much less interested researchers involved in the technical debate, some of whom may be genuinely 'agnostic', but the pace of the argument is sustained by those fellow scientists who act as advocates. With no possibility of consensus on any technical point which might be useful to policymakers, decisions are of necessity made largely independently of the often huge body of literature produced by the rival armies of technical experts. Policy is made which is a compromise between the competing parties in the time-honoured way, everyone gaining a little and losing something as well. Compromise of this sort requires next to nothing by way of technical information. In short, policy resulting from compromise is quite insensitive to any scientific claims made in the technical debate, which is just as well given the discussion in the previous chapter. Rather than science being a natural servant to the needs of policy, there is a fundamental antagonism between them, relevance to policy effectively destroying the conditions under which technical consensus may be expected.

The above description of the relationship between science and policy will be known as the over-critical model, and it is summed up in Figure 1. The sceptical hypothesis, that all attempts by science to make a significant impact on policy came to grief in the way described by the over-critical model,

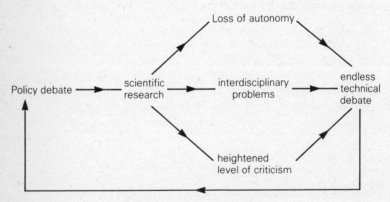

Figure 1 *The Over-critical Model*

may now be tested against a number of case studies. The first, concerning the control of lead pollution, is more extensive than the others, containing an extended discussion of policy as well as an analysis of the technical controversy.

The reader may now be a little wary: surely too much is being claimed; doubt is one thing, unbridled scepticism another. No doubt many cases will come to mind where science seems happily applied to practical questions of policy without the endless disputation claimed by the over-critical model. The key to the problem is the measurement of the sensitivity of policy to a conjecture by that hypothesis' error cost, and the recognition that the level of criticism a hypothesis receives ought to increase with its error cost. This prevents science having any great influence on the direction of policy; great influence for a conjecture implies a high error cost which, in turn, will ensure that the conjecture is submitted to intense critical scrutiny, destroying any hope of agreement about its acceptability. But this leaves room for many cases where the influence of science is real but none the less very slight. Put formally, policy is insensitive to a scientific conjecture which may therefore possess such a low error cost that it can be accepted by all scientists without endless disagreement, being subject to only a modest level of criticism. The sceptical thesis concerns the ability of science to have more than a very modest influence upon political choices.

A limiting case of modesty, which will be called the under-critical model (see Figure 2), arises where an existing

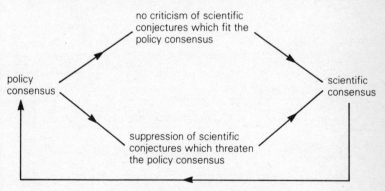

Figure 2 *The Under-critical Model*

consensus on policy ensures a ready, uncritical reception of whatever scientific claims appear to support the policy. In such a case, science is used to legitimate or rationalize political choices which have already been taken, but the price of easy acceptance is the impossibility of influencing policy. Scientific conjectures function here in a political way, to deepen the already existing agreement about policy, for dissenters must now overcome science as well as their usual political adversaries.

Moreover, in these cases the scientific hypotheses concerned have a zero error cost. Believing them, policy is this, disbelieving them, policy is just the same, giving the political choice zero sensitivity to the conjectures. Not surprisingly, the conjectures are subject to no real criticism at all. There are many cases where science seems to inform policy without degenerating into the endless dissension of the over-critical model, but on closer inspection an approximation to the under-critical model will be found where the influence of science is wholly spurious. The over-critical model rules out cases where a scientific conjecture has a high error cost or, in other words, policy is sensitive to a conjecture, and where there is a technical consensus about the acceptance of the conjecture, and it is through this prohibition that the model will be tested in what follows.

5 Lead—The Technical Debate

Having described the sceptical hypothesis which is to be tested, the first case study against which it may be measured concerns policy towards the control of lead in the environment. In this chapter we will consider the structure of the technical debate which is still continuing between scientists who take very different views of the problem posed by environmental levels of lead, some claiming it to be highly damaging to young children, others that it is quite harmless. It will be shown that the over-critical model fits the case very well: loss of autonomy, interdisciplinary research and a rise in the level of criticism to which conjectures are subjected combining to give a potentially endless debate between scientists. Research does not limit the political argument about what to do about lead pollution, which is the intention, rather, the policy conflict generates a matching conflict of a technical nature. The consequences of the over-critical model for policymaking are then considered in the following two chapters, the first of these attacking rational or synoptic conceptions of policymaking which give great prominence to scientific advice in the formulation of policy. If the case of lead is at all typical, policy can hardly rely on scientific research, which never seems to approach consensus. The final chapter dealing with lead hopes to be more positive, describing how policy can be made in cases like the present one where scientific advice degenerates into endless technical bickering. Material for the case study is drawn largely from British and American sources.

Loss of Autonomy

The problems associated with the departure from autonomy are well displayed by research into the dose-response relationships of lead in humans, and in particular in children. This topic has only been researched because of its relevance to policy, for it is clear that science under autonomous control would never have investigated this little corner at this time.

There is at present no adequate measure for lead dose (Environmental Protection Agency 1977, 1-330-4). Blood lead concentrations are generally used for this purpose, although their shortcomings are well known. Blood lead equilibrates with the rest of the body over a period of a few weeks, and so measures exposure to the metal over this period. It is therefore quite possible to find people with the same blood lead level today who have radically different histories of exposure. One person might have received only normal exposure, and one severely damaging exposure many years previously, which no longer shows up in the blood. Lead in milk teeth has also been used as a measure of exposure, but has a similar failing, being a reflection of exposure integrated over the child's lifetime and blurring out the peaks of exposure which are likely to have caused the most harm to the child.

Whatever tissue is used, moreover, there are very serious problems attached to chemical analysis, great care being needed (Sherlock *et al.* 1985). Cross-laboratory calibration of measuring instruments is both difficult and time-consuming and is often a source of major error. This means that although the results of blood or tooth lead levels in one study may be acceptable as relative measures, they cannot be compared in any direct way with results published from other laboratories. The response of humans, and especially children, to doses of lead is also very hard to characterize, given the great complexity of the human nervous system which takes years to reach maturity. This leaves open the possibility that deficits due to lead may only appear in a detectable form some years later, confusing the experimental search for damage from exposure to lead. There is also, of course, the added complication that humans cannot be experimented on. It is not possible to dose children with lead and to watch their development; whatever experiments of this type are done are therefore adventitious. To give just one example of the limitations this places on research, the proportion of lead in food and drink which is absorbed by infants is a key problem for research which hopes to inform policy, but Collingridge and Douglas (1984) point out that ethical restrictions on experimenting with children mean that there are very few studies on this topic; those that exist use a handful of children who have accidentally taken in large quantities of lead. There is no consensus on the fraction of lead which is absorbed, although food and drink probably account for 80 per cent of a typical child's total exposure to the metal. Whether children absorb 8 per cent, or whether they absorb 40 per cent of the lead in their diet, the consequences for policy are obviously profound.

Enough has been said to show that scientists under autonomous control would never have chosen the dose-response relationship of lead in humans as a research topic. If they hoped to work towards an understanding of the relationship, they would first have chosen an animal subject with a short life, a simple nervous system and free of ethical restraints on experiment. Only when the questions posed by such animals had been solved would any attempt have been made to understand the human subject. Concern for policy has in this case made scientists tackle problems whose solution is too difficult in the present state of the art. Research on lead therefore tends to be of poor quality, a failing which makes it particularly easy to criticize whatever findings appear in the literature if they seem to support an unwelcome policy option. Science is, of course, highly competitive, and if one researcher forbears from obtaining money to research on some aspect of the lead problem relevant to policy—thinking it beyond the powers of his discipline in its present state of development—some less scrupulous, or more optimistic, rival is sure to step in. Practitioners find it difficult to estimate their discipline's power to answer questions posed from outside, and error, as in any competitive enterprise, always errs towards optimism.

Interdisciplinary Problems

The conflict between Patterson, the geochemist, and the industrial hygienists working on lead has been briefly described in Chapter 3, and is a reminder that research on the health effects of lead is often beset by similar confusions, misunderstandings and territorial violence. The technical questions raised by concern over the control of environmental lead do not fall into one or two neat disciplinary boxes; it is often far from obvious which disciplines might be able to tackle a particular problem. The resulting competition between disciplines exacerbates the problems associated with communicating across disciplinary divides. Autonomous science is occasionally bedevilled by similar problems where practitioners from a range of disciplines must work on the same problem, but this is a rarity, and should interdisciplinary confusions proliferate, the puzzle may be taken off the scientific agenda at not too great a cost. It is quite otherwise, of course, with the work on lead which is supposed to inform the choices of policymakers, where the cost of delay will be very great.

A second example of interdisciplinary problems is discussed in Collingridge (1980) and concerns the lengthy row between the United States Environmental Protection Agency (EPA) and a major American manufacturer of lead additives for petrol, the Ethyl Corporation, over the health effects on children of lead from vehicle exhausts. A central argument of the EPA was that although there was no statistically significant correlation between air lead concentrations and the blood lead level of people breathing such air, broad differences between blood lead levels in cities and suburbs indicated that removing lead from petrol would reduce the health risks associated with the metal. Against this, the Ethyl Corporation argued that lead from petrol should be viewed as innocent until proved guilty, by studies which show with the customary 95 per cent confidence that there is a link between blood and air lead levels. Each side is tacitly employing quite different standards about the amount of evidence required before a decision can be made. EPA employs standards more familiar to medical disciplines where choices have routinely to be made in the absence of evidence, where the Ethyl Corporation employs a standard drawn from pure science in which the luxury of delaying action until sufficient evidence is accumulated can often be afforded. Had the standards been stated explicitly, the nature of the disagreement might have been clearer, but throughout the debate they remained tacit and therefore a source of confusion and misunderstanding. Thus the Ethyl Corporation constantly criticized EPA on the grounds that it had not proved its assertion that removing lead from petrol would lower blood lead levels in the population;

the rejoinder was a repetition of the original evidence—the broad blood lead differences in urban–suburban populations.

A more recent example of interdisciplinary problems comes from Britain where the Lawther Report (Department of Health and Social Security 1980), sponsored by the Government and written by a panel of scientists, none of whom were experienced in animal studies or biochemisty, reviewed the evidence on the toxicity of lead in the environment and in doing so rejected all animal studies as irrelevant to an understanding of the medical effects of lead on humans. The answering report, Conservation Society (1980), criticized Lawther for this omission, and referred to animal studies and biochemical studies in defending its case for an immediate ban on lead in petrol and for other strict controls. If these studies are relevant to humans, it would appear that present lead levels in the environment are seriously damaging to children; if they are not, then Lawther's opinion stands that the evidence is equivocal and more research is needed before policy conclusions can be drawn. But in science there is no way of deciding the relevance of such findings in one area to those in another. No routine application of scientific method, standard test or experiment can settle the issue. Those who wish to ban lead obviously favour animal and biochemical studies as being relevant, and their opponents favour the contrary, but how is the question to be brought beyond prejudice to rational assessment?

Raising the Level of Criticism

Policy distorts the processes which make pure science such a powerful instrument by destroying autonomy, imposing external aims on the normal goals of scientific puzzle-solving, and forcing research to be interdisciplinary, with all the pitfalls which that entails. A third effect will now be examined: the raising of the level of criticism. In pure science, remote from any contamination by real-world policy, the cost of errors is low and therefore a low degree of criticism is appropriate. Where error is inexpensive, it does not make sense to expend huge quantities of energy in their discovery and many rival conjectures may be maintained at any time with little incentive to choose the one best theory. Where science bears on policy, things change dramatically. The cost of errors may make a qualitative leap, for mistakes are no longer confined to the laboratory but may mean life or death for millions of people. Since errors are now so expensive, it is appropriate to search diligently for them—a much more critical attitude than that found in pure science. This increase in the level of criticism is very clear throughout the whole of the current debate about the health effects of lead; we have space, however, for only a couple of examples from the rich store which it provides. In the debate between EPA and the Ethyl Corporation, if the case that lead in petrol poisons children is accepted when it is, in fact, false, the error costs fall to the Corporation and the lead industry generally, which will suffer a severe loss of business, with no gains at all. The Corporation is therefore highly critical, and quite rightly so, of scientific reports which seem to show that lead is a poison. By the same token, EPA is highly critical of research results which appear to show that lead from petrol is harmless, for if such results are accepted while being false EPA will have failed in its duty to protect millions of children from poisoning. In this case EPA bears the error cost and therefore scrutinizes such results with great zeal. If the same technical questions were posed in pure science, there might be room for compromise—agreement that both sides had something to say and that further research must be done before the matter could be settled—but the relevance of these results to policy makes this quite impossible. It must be stressed that the increase in the level of criticism between EPA and the Ethyl Corporation is a rational feature of debate. Neither side is distorting scientific method to protect its own interests, they are, on the contrary, exercising their right to argue against conjectures which have a great bearing on their own well-being.

It is clear from the description of the debate given by Collingridge (1980) that there was never the remotest chance of agreement between EPA and the Ethyl Corporation on any substantial point, despite the enormous technical range of the argument. Both sides operated double standards, being highly critical of scientific reports which threatened their position, but quite uncritical of supporting findings. There was therefore very little change in the positions of the two parties in the light of criticism. It is clear that any scientific conjecture which was thought to be important in the debate was subject to intense critical scrutiny from one side or the other. It might be thought that the legal framework of the argument made each side over-state its case in this way, but exactly the same features are in fact demonstrated by the more recent British debate between the Lawther Report and the Conservation Society, alluded to earlier, where there are no legal entanglements. As before, scientific evidence which supports the case of one side is care-fully extracted from the enormous body of literature which is now available. Each side is quite uncritical of supporting evidence and highly critical of findings which threaten to under-mine its case. In this way, any conjecture which is of more than marginal importance in the debate is submitted, by one side or the other, to a much more intense critical scrutiny than it would receive as a conjecture of pure science.

Endless Debate

The three features described above conspire to prevent any significant contribution from the huge amount of scientific research on lead to improvements in policies for the control of environmental lead. As science becomes involved in policy questions, the cost of error makes a quantum leap, with a con-sequent rise in the temperature of criticism. People engaged in the policy debate wish to be critical of scientific results which might threaten them, and not only is this their perfect right, but criticism becomes particularly easy because of the poor qual-ity of research and the interdisciplinary problems associated with it. The result is the apparently endless technical debate which surrounds the health effects of lead. Instead of scientific research reducing the extent of disagreement over policy, the political conflict generates a persistent technical one. Research in the early 1960s shattered the complacency that accompanied the domination of research into lead by indus-trial hygienists. This work created uncertainty about the toxi-city of environmental levels of lead, but all the massive research effort which has followed since then has been unable to resolve this uncertainty. In this case, therefore, whatever happens in others, science is a generator of uncertainty, not a suppressor. Four features of the lead debate are worth particular attention: technical questions cannot be answered despite the vast quantities of data which are available, making a very wide range of technical opinion possible; many long-settled technical questions are reopened; attempts to settle one technical issue generally succeed only in introducing a whole number of additional issues, widening the debate still further, and both sides practise selective citation.

The first point is well illustrated by the debate between EPA and the Ethyl Corporation about the health effects of lead in petrol. EPA (1972) is the original statement of the case for regulation, based on the following technical claims, as formulated in Collingridge (1980).

1. Since lead has not been shown to have any biologically useful function in the body any increase in body burden of lead is accompanied by an increased risk of human health impairment.
2. In many cities air lead concentrations are slowly rising.
3. Human blood lead levels begin to rise appreciably with an exposure to airborne lead concentrations in excess of 2 micrograms per cubic metre.
4. Elevated lead intake for periods as short as three months produces an increase in blood lead levels.
5. Body burdens of lead increase with age, at least to forty years and probably thereafter.
6. Although the ingestion of leaded paint is the predominant cause of lead poisoning in children, some children may show high blood lead levels from the ingestion of dust contaminated by fall-out from airborne lead.
7. Average blood levels tend to be higher among urban residents than among rural residents and higher among groups occupationally exposed to vehicle exhaust (e.g. policemen and garage workmen).

These claims were supported by an impressive body of research data, particularly the National Academy of Sciences (1971), and yet every one of EPA's points were challenged by Ethyl Corporation (1972) whose arguments may be summarized thus:

Against 1. Years of experience with occupationally exposed groups show blood lead levels well in excess of those found in the normally exposed population to be perfectly safe.

Against 2. The evidence indicates that air lead concentrations in many cities are falling. American blood leads are of the same order as those for many non-industrialized populations, indicating that lead from industrial sources makes only a small contribution to blood lead levels.

Against 3. The data used in the calculation of this 2.0 microgram per cubic metre limit is seriously suspect, as is the statistical device used in the calculation. More reliable data (the so-called 7 City Study) shows no correlation between air lead levels and blood lead levels. In addition, the EPA assumed that about 30 per cent of lead inhaled is retained in the lung. The true figure is nearer 10 per cent.

Against 4. This may be the case, but there is no evidence to indicate that the 'excess' blood lead levels resulting from exposure to airborne lead are a health hazard.

Against 5. The data on body burdens show that lead body burdens do not increase with age. Even if they do, this would merely reflect the very long time (about thirty years) needed for the body to come into equilibrium with environmental lead.

Against 6. There is no known correlation between lead levels in dust and earth and blood lead levels of children exposed to the dust and earth. There is no evidence whatever for EPA's hypothesis about dust being a significant contributor to the blood lead of children. The rate of lead fall-out is so low that this can only be an insignificant source of lead.

Against 7. The very large 7 City Study reveals no correlation between air lead levels and blood lead levels.

The Ethyl Corporation extended its case by arguing that EPA's proposed regulations would be much more expensive to implement than they had originally calculated, with adverse environmental effects—changes in refining practices required to make the low lead fuel increasing the amount of hazardous hydrocarbons emitted.

EPA (1973a) not only revised the regulations, but also changed the case for reducing lead levels in petrol. The new case drops items 2 to 5 from the argument, the most important being 3, the claim that blood lead levels rise on exposure to air containing more than $2\mu g/m^3$ of lead, which had been savagely attacked by the Corporation. Claims 1, 6 and 7 are strenuously restated, however, the last being supported by new evidence available from the 7 City Survey. But the removal of items 2 to 5 is hardly a victory for the Ethyl Corporation, for the EPA had other arguments for its regulations, indeed it is the existence of these other arguments which gave the EPA the freedom to change their original case. The new claims are:

8. Many city dwellers have abnormally high blood lead levels.
9. The susceptibility of children may be greater than adults so that children may be suffering subtle but unrecognized neurological impairment due to lead.
10. Newborn babies in cities have higher blood lead levels than newborn babies in rural areas.
11. Chromosomal damage due to lead is possible.
12. The lowest blood lead level at which the health of some expectant mothers (newborn child, child, adult) is impaired is 30 (30, 40, 40) micrograms per 100 ml.

Ethyl Corporation (1973) countered by arguing:

Against 8. The upper level for city dwellers' blood lead is around 40 micrograms per 100 ml which cannot be said to be 'abnormal'. Many higher values turn out to be the result of faulty analysis. For children, high blood leads are solely due to exposure to leaded paints.

Against 9. The major evidence for this is the work of David. Other investigations have failed to discover the same effect. David's results were due to the higher incidence of pica (the habitual eating of curious substances, often including lead paint) in hyperactive children.

Against 10. This claim is in direct contradiction to the paper cited by the EPA.

Against 11. The evidence for such chromosomal damage is extremely speculative.

Against 12. This claim is supported by no evidence. It is an *ad hoc* redefinition of upper acceptable blood lead level by EPA.

Item 6 is also undermined, the Corporation argues, by a survey of lead poisoning in children which failed to find a single instance of dust as a source of the poison. Experiments on animals seem to show that lead is, after all, an essential element, contrary to EPA's item 1.

Round three of the debate was EPA's publication of EPA (1973b) in support of their final proposed regulations. Unlike earlier documents this one was not open to review. Nevertheless, EPA's case had changed significantly from the second round, in three ways. No evidence was given for children having the previously supposed greater susceptibility to lead poisoning: their special position is now based on their greater exposure to other sources of lead, in dust and paint. Secondly, the same upper acceptable blood lead level is now attributed to expectant mothers and newborn infants, as to others, at $40\mu g/100$ ml. Finally, the reality of the correlation between blood lead and air lead levels is restated. Another new element was the model of a standard man exposed to various sources of lead, showing, or so it was claimed, that to keep below the upper acceptable blood lead level, the population should be exposed to air containing below $11.8\mu g/m^3$ on optimistic assumptions, and below $4.0\mu g/m^3$ on pessimistic ones.

The final round was the inevitable court case, about which we need say little, except that EPA eventually won its case: the regulations it had fought so hard for are now in force. Looking at the various rounds of the argument, it is clear that both sides set out to build up the best technical case they could—EPA to the effect that lead from vehicles is poisonous, the Ethyl Corporation to the contrary. Scientific evidence which fits the case is cited without criticism, while that which undermines the case is subject to the most intense scrutiny. This is not too difficult, for there is a huge technical literature available to those opposing the case, covering many disciplines which can be dipped into as needed. There is therefore ample room for each side to build up a case, changing it as time goes on, as new reports supplement the stock of literature and in response to one's opponent's criticisms. With such opportunities, there is no possibility of one side losing to the other, having to accept on scientific grounds the technical case made out by its rival. EPA changed its case and dropped various claims, but only because there were others to take their place. Had the claims been essential to the Agency's case, things would have gone very differently. Things are made even easier by the poor quality of much of the research on lead, as mentioned earlier, which leave it open to criticism if this is needed, and the interdisciplinarity of the problem which opens even more opportunities for criticism.

The EPA's job is not to make a dispassionate survey of the technical literature on the health effects of vehicle exhausts, but to make out the best case it can for action, just as the Corporation has to attack the Agency's case as best it can. Given the limitations of the data available, the kind of debate described above is therefore inevitable. The technical question as to whether lead from vehicle exhausts harms children is therefore not answerable from the debate. In the present case the courts stepped in, but in their absence it is clear that the arguments could have continued indefinitely; indeed, many of the points of contention are still being debated ten years later, such as the effect of airborne fall-out from vehicle exhausts on lead in food and drink, and the association of blood lead and air levels. To say that conflicts such as the debate about the health effects of lead in petrol are highly resistant to data is an understatement.

Comparison with the British debate over the Lawther Report will once again dispel fears that the peculiar features of the lead debate discussed above are due to the legal framework which was eventually forced on to it. The working party of the Department of Health and Social Security under Professor Lawther consisted of 'independent experts actively engaged in the fields of clinical paediatrics, pathology, child psychiatry, psychology, epidemiology and the environmental sciences', with the remit of reviewing the evidence on the health effects of lead and making recommendations about policy in the light of it. The report emphasizes the uncertainties involved and the patchy nature of the evidence available, particularly about health effects of low levels of lead. The contributors nevertheless conclude that about 90 per cent of lead in the body of the typical Briton comes from his/her diet, overwhelmingly from food, and only 10 per cent comes from the air—90 per cent of this arising from vehicle exhausts. There are local 'hot spots' where water and air provide much greater contributions, and the report recommends various local actions in such circumstances, but this is the general picture. Much remains to be discovered about the effects of low levels of lead on children, but it can be said that there is no conclusive evidence for any harm below a blood lead level of 35μg/100 ml, and that clinical poisoning can occur at above 80μg/100 ml. Between these two figures lies an area of great uncertainty.

Policies recommended by the Lawther Report cover those directed at hot spots and a number aimed at lowering normal levels of lead, such as a steady reduction in the lead levels permitted in food and drink and in domestic water supplies. Levels allowed in petrol should be limited to ensure that concentrations of lead in air in places where people are regularly exposed are below 2μg/m³. The Conservation Society was very disappointed with such modest proposals and attacked the Lawther Report in its own report, Conservation Society (1980). One criticism of the Lawther Report has already been considered, Lawther's disregard of biochemical and animal studies, which the Conservation Society argue reveals an effect on children at a blood lead level as low as 5μg/100 ml, putting in doubt any idea of a threshold. The second major criticism is that the Lawther Report fails to recognize that lead from petrol is a major source of the metal since fall-out from vehicles contaminates crops, soil, eating utensils and fingers, so much so as to make it the major source of lead in the diet. Much stricter controls on lead are therefore called for: the complete removal of lead from petrol within a year; the prohibition of the use of lead in any food processing and in printer's ink, lubricants and cosmetics; with a reduction in the maximum permitted airborne lead in industry from 150 to 10μg/m³ by 1984. All the features of the earlier American debate are mirrored here. Both sides accept evidence which fits their own views on policy, that of the safe government experts of the Lawther Committee, and the environmental crusaders of the Conservation Society.

The second notable feature of the lead debate is that many technical questions which were thought to have been settled long ago are now opened. We have already seen examples of this with Patterson's questioning of the long-established idea of the threshold for lead poisoning and the high level of lead in pre-industrial times, and with the EPA's undermining of the equally august consensus that lead from food is the chief source of exposure for humans, with the argument that much of this lead comes from vehicle exhaust spread to crops and hence to the home. The third point, related to this, is that attempts to close one technical issue usually succeed merely in opening up a whole number of further issues for debate. Instead of the technical debate narrowing down to fewer and fewer items of dissent as new evidence becomes available, adding further evidence raises the number of issues under discussion. A recent example is the famous Turin Study where lead with an unusual ratio of two isotopes was added to petrol throughout Piedmont in Italy for two years, the change in the isotope ratio of lead in the blood of residents being monitored to give an estimate for the contribution of lead from this source to blood lead. On all counts, the experiment was judged of brilliant design, powerful enough to settle the vexed technical question which had so often been debated in the past with inadequate evidence. But once the study's results were in print, disappointment replaced hope as its technical quality and the typicality of the city of Turin came under fire in, for example, Elwood (1983, 1984). Attempts to close the issue of the contribution of lead in petrol to blood lead merely succeeded in opening up a further set of questions: is the epidemiology of the Turin study adequate and in any case is Turin at all typical of cities? Instead of reducing the ground for dissent, research succeeds only in widening the debate.

Selective citation is revealed in the extraordinary citation pattern which Reeve (1985) observes in the contending reports of Lawther (Department of Health and Social Security 1980), and the Conservation Society (1980). Of the 276 papers cited in the Conservation Society Report and the 125 by Lawther, only thirty are cited by both. Thus, out of 371 papers cited, only thirty were cited by both parties. Nineteen papers are cited at least four times by the Conservation Society, and fifteen by Lawther, but of these only one is common. Thus, of the thirty-three highly cited papers, only one is highly cited in both reports. While too much importance must not be placed on such crude data, it is clear that each side selectively cites evidence which supports its case, and criticizes—by neglect—evidence which supports the case of its opponent.

The conclusion of this chapter is that the case of lead fits the over-critical model very well. Scientific research is drawn very far from its autonomous path in trying to help policymakers, and the poor quality of work which results is compounded by the confusions and misunderstandings inevitably associated with interdisciplinary research in science. Relevance to policy produces a qualitative change in the error cost associated with conjectures about the health effects of the metal, generating a much sterner critical regime than any found in pure science. People involved in the debate wish to be critical, and the poor quality of the research work makes this particularly easy. The technical debate produced by this combination of failings threatens to be interminable. Despite huge quantities of data, there are no answers to technical questions relevant to policy, and instead of narrowing as more research is produced, the debate widens to cover more and more issues. Scientists engaged in the argument, or at least some of them, are best seen as advocates, seeking not to give an independent, objective, neutral, unbiased assessment of the entire literature within their competence, but rather scouring the literature for data which can be put together to make a case in support of the political interests they serve, through employment, professionalization or personal inclination. The existence of such a debate obviously calls into question the relevance of all this body of research to policy—a point to be explored in the next two chapters.

6 Lead—Myths of Policymaking

The myth of information discussed in Chapter 1 holds that information is the essential ingredient of good decision-making, and the myth is at its most elaborate when it is assumed that anything short of full, total information must lead to poor, essentially arbitrary choices. According to the ideals of synoptic rationality, a full overview of the choices available is to be aimed at, even though this may often be hard, or even impossible, to achieve in practice. The present chapter will consider the suitability of the synoptic ideal in determining policy on lead pollution, arguing that it makes quite impossible demands, particularly on science which is supposed to provide the mass of information needed for a synoptic view in this case. Given the analysis of the lead debate offered in the previous chapter, there is clearly something profoundly wrong with a conception of the policy process which attaches such importance to the gathering of an enormous number of scientific findings. Readers already convinced of the frailty of synoptic rationality and whose views need no further reinforcement will miss little by omitting the present chapter which relies heavily on Collingridge and Douglas (1984).

A Synoptic View Attempted

In terms of synoptic rationality, a policymaker ought to achieve a synoptic view of the problem before coming to a decision, identifying which values are relevant to the problem in hand, and undertaking a comprehensive survey of all possible means of furthering these values. All the consequences, or likely consequences, of adopting each of these means should be exhaustively listed, so that a decision can be made which maximizes the attainment of the policymaker's values. There are many variations on this theme: some insist that cost-benefit calculations be done, some that cardinal utility calculations be done; some require maximization of benefit, while others employ the weaker idea of satisficing. But as Carley (1980) points out, there is more uniting these variations than separating them: in particular, the demand for a thorough review of relevant values, and of courses of actions which are open and their likely consequences. Collingridge (1982) shows that such a synoptic view can be achieved only for fairly humble decisions, but it is nevertheless frequently appealed to as an ideal to which policymakers should aspire. In considering the practicality of achieving a synoptic view of the hazard posed by lead in the environment and of ways of controlling it, the recent report by the US National Research Council (NRC, 1980), *Lead in the Human Environment*, is useful. The report's authors do not achieve a synoptic view of their problem, for this is obstructed by many uncertainties, but they are convinced that such a view is required to resolve the lead problem and that it is well worth working towards its achievement. In other words, they take the synoptic view as an ideal to which policymakers concerned with lead (and by implication all policymakers) should aim.

The NRC study had two purposes: to assess current knowledge about the various hazards from lead and ways of controlling them, and to recommend research priorities 'for obtaining information needed to support rational decisions' (p. 13). In seeking to provide a list of uncertainties which need to be resolved through research so that rational decisions may be made, the report's authors clearly need some view of a rational decision-making model is explicitly stated, and con-assumption that rationality requires a synoptic view to be taken of the problem at hand. As far as lead is concerned, a rational decision-making model is explicitly stated, and consists of the following steps (p. 15):

1. Identify sources of lead and pathways of environmental transfer.
2. Identify specific human populations with exposures to lead.
3. Estimate the level of exposure to lead by each environmental pathway for each specific population.
4. Establish the association between exposure to lead and the level of lead in the body for each specific population.
5. Establish the association between the level of lead in the body and biological change due to lead for each specific population.
6. Estimate the upper limit of non-detrimental biological change for each specific population and the level of lead in the body associated with that degree of biological change.

7. Identify and describe alternative control strategies.
8. Apply risk-benefit, cost-benefit, and other considerations, compare alternatives for control, and decide what is an acceptable level of lead in the environment for each specific population.
9. Evaluate the process and the decision.

   Lindblom (1965, 1968, 1979) and Braybrooke and Lindblom (1963) have made a number of general criticisms of the synoptic ideal, and we shall now consider how these 'score' against the NRC's report, paying particular attention to the role assigned to experts and technical findings in policymaking.
(a) The deepest criticism concerns the assumption that the problems of controlling lead hazards can be resolved by further scientific research. The report adopts a very simple-minded view of scientific knowledge which gives rise to this assumption. 'Scientific knowledge', we are told, 'includes both data and an understanding of scientific concepts, principles, and methods, that permits meaningful interpretations of data' (p. 49). Notice that nothing has been said about the 'meaningful interpretation of data'. It is assumed throughout the report that wherever questions arise about how to interpret a particular body of data, these can be resolved by the collection of more data. The collection of adequate data 'minimizes the selective use of information to support preconceived conclusions' (p. 14). But what the earlier discussion about the current debate over lead hazards shows above all is that it is not amenable to resolution by the gathering in of more and more experimental findings. The problem, quite unrecognized in the NRC report, is that these findings need to be interpreted in some way, and that there is more freedom in interpretation than in accepting the data themselves. Opposing sides in the lead debate accept the experimental data, but they choose to put quite different interpretations upon them, all of which are consistent with the data and with scientific method. Argument about rival interpretations suggests further experiments to help settle the issues, but when these have been carried out, the need for interpretation arises once again, so that the findings are much less decisive and univocal than had been hoped, and so the story continues. Thus, as experimental findings have

increased, the debate has proliferated instead of focusing down on a narrow range of uncertainties. There are, however, further secondary reasons for the failure of synoptic rationality which are of some interest.

(b) The NRC report issues a list of research which needs to be undertaken if present knowledge is to be expanded sufficiently to provide a synoptic view of the lead problem, and categorizes them as high, medium and low priority. Confined to short-term, high-priority, scientific research, the list is impressive enough (pp. 256–60):

1. Epidemiological studies of populations, including biochemical and functional tests on individuals, representing the full range of current typical exposure to lead.
2. Toxicological research on effects of lead, at doses corresponding to commonplace exposures, on biochemical and physiological functions of cells and animals, with special emphasis on the delineation of biological changes that may be precursors of pathophysiological processes.
3. Pharmacodynamic investigations of the absorption, distribution, storage, mobilization, excretion, and homeostatic regulation of lead in humans.
4. Studies to define more precisely the nature and extent of heightened susceptibility to lead toxicity during the pre- and perinatal periods and the first few years of life, especially in terms of the developing nervous system and behaviour.
5. Studies to define more precisely the relationships between timing of doses and effects, and especially the relative hazards of single or infrequent high exposures compared to chronic, lower levels of exposure to lead.
6. Studies to examine empirical multiple statistical regressions among indices of lead in the body (e.g. blood lead, dentine lead) and measured levels of lead in the air, water, foods, soil, paint, dust, and other possible contributing sources.
7. Extensive data gathering on the levels and chemical/physical properties of lead in specific foods, water supplies, gasoline, soils, dusts, and paints and in people; on dietary and liquid consumption patterns and soil, dust, or paint ingestion tendencies of individuals and groups; and on relationships between ingestion and excretion of lead in various source materials.
8. Continued development of general models of source contributions, environmental mass-balance estimates, and other frameworks for integrating the information.

9. Information is needed on trends in blood levels and other indexes of lead in the body, and better definitions of the statistical distribution of individual values in specific populations are essential for standard-setting purposes.
10. Better definition of the unique chemical and physical characteristics of lead in various environmental pools, and increased attention to the usefulness of specific aspects of these properties in identifying sources and measuring transfer processes.
11. Effective development and dissemination of techniques for preventing lead contamination of samples, equipment, and reagents.
12. Improved standard reference materials for lead in environmental samples and biological fluids and tissues.

Each of these items is a research programme, rather than a well-defined topic. The quantity of research required, even for the above list, is extraordinary even if we take a conventional view of the power of science to reach consensus about such issues. This takes us straight to one of Lindblom's central criticisms of the synoptic ideal: that its achievement requires so much information that it is simply too expensive to reach.

(c) The report's authors are realistic in observing that there is little hope of a major expansion in research funding for the research priorities it identifies. This means that, even if we accept the report's rather simple-minded view of science, it will be many years before all this research is done. If a more realistic view of scientific progress is taken then the resolution of the uncertainties which currently prevent the adoption of a synoptic view will be an even longer affair. This may not appear too serious a problem since, after all, the results produced by even a limited research effort on lead will be valuable by themselves. But this is to overlook a serious drawback to the synoptic ideal recognized by Lindblom. Generally speaking, the value of a given research finding on lead will be highly dependent on what other research findings have been acquired. It is well known, for example, that lead exists in many chemical forms in food and that some of these will be transformed by reactions in the gastro-intestinal tract, but detailed knowledge is limited at present. Different forms of lead can be expected to have different rates of absorption in the gastro-intestinal tract. An understanding of the contribution to body burden made by lead from a particular food therefore calls for knowledge of both the chemical composition of the lead and the absorption rate of that form of the metal. Knowledge of one without the other is valueless in furthering the understanding of sources of lead in the body and ways of reducing lead burdens. What this means is that very often a great deal of information must be acquired before any individual items become of any value.

(d) The picture of rational policymaking about lead painted by the report is therefore one of the slow and steady accumulation of research findings, which by themselves have limited value, but which eventually enable a synoptic view of the lead problem to be taken that is highly valuable for the formulation of policy. It will take many years for this view to emerge; what is to be done during this interim period? This is a particular case of Lindblom's general point that the synoptic ideal is in fact empty because it gives no guidance on how to make decisions when the ideal cannot be met. The synoptic ideal tells us only to work on and acquire all the information which it needs. The ideal says nothing about how decisions on the control of lead hazards are to be made in the interim before all this information is to hand. Such choices can only be arbitrary. The decision-maker is supposed to use 'best-guess' estimates for critical variables where knowledge is weak (p. 100), but calling these 'best guesses' is simply an attempt to disguise their arbitrariness—a 'best guess' in the absence of information is simply a guess. A decision based on such a guess is as arbitrary as the guess itself. Thus Lindblom enables us to identify another cost of the synoptic ideal. Information itself is expensive, but to this may now be added the cost of arbitrary decision-making throughout the period needed to give sufficient information for a synoptic view.

(e) Lindblom has observed how the nature of policy questions can vary in a shorter time than a synoptic view of the problem can be achieved, so that research often turns out to provide answers to yesterday's policy questions. This is true of the present example. The problem of lead in the environment is an ever-changing one: lead pigments in paint have gradually been superseded by zinc and titanium pigments, Edwards (1980) discusses the technology of canning which will soon provide cheaper cans than those of today which require lead solders. Substitutes for scarce petroleum may eventually produce an unleaded internal combustion fuel; changes in treatment of water affect lead pick-up in domestic supplies, and so on. Some of these are long-term changes, but others occur much more quickly. Policymakers, and hence their expert advisers, are therefore directing controls towards moving targets, and this must be recognized in directing the research programme on lead. It is no use discovering the exact chemical forms of lead in canned foods, their absorption rate in the body, and contribution to burdens of lead in various organs, if by the time this difficult and complex research has been completed canning practices have changed and lead is no longer a contaminant. With the very long, large-scale research programme envisaged by the NRC's report this is bound to happen time and again. The report recognizes the need for periodic reviews of research priorities (p. 263), but quite fails to appreciate that very often the problem will have been found to have changed long before the research aimed at solving it has been completed.

The same blindness to the mutability of political goals is behind the report's failure to understand the necessity for the political feasibility of controls on lead. Ashby and Anderson (1981) remind us that controls on environmental lead must be practicable given the present political situation, and they must be policeable if they are to be effective. This is recognized in the report, but only in passing. Its importance is greatly underplayed because of the report's concentration on limits rather than controls. Determining an upper acceptable limit for lead in, say, the air, is to calculate the air lead level below which no one in the target population will suffer an impairment of health. This is largely a technical matter, and clearly has nothing to do with political feasibility. If the slightest trace of lead in air is harmful to someone, then this is so whether achieving lead-free air is a practical possibility or not. Issues of politics arise when controls are considered—when, for example, ways of ensuring that air lead levels do not exceed the upper acceptable limit have to be found. Whatever action is taken (against motorists, petrol refiners, lead smelters, or whoever), the action has to be within the bounds of political possibility, and it has to be enforceable in some way. In the real world, this may limit the options which are open to such an extent that a great deal of the research proposed by the NRC is beside the point. For example, canned food is a major source of dietary lead, but according to Edwards (1980), in practice there are few controls which can be placed on it. Researching into the chemical composition of lead in canned food, the absorption rates of its various forms and their effect in the body, and toxicity, are therefore largely irrelevant to the problem of controlling lead hazards.

(f) A further point about the NRC's reliance on experts, mentioned in the previous chapter, is that many of the unknown factors preventing the achievement of a synoptic view can only be resolved by experiments which are unethical. Knowledge of the respiratory and gastro-intestinal absorption of lead by children is central to the synoptic view sought by the NRC, but is severely hampered by ethical restrictions on exposing children to damaging substances. With these limitations, the research may take many decades, or may never be carried out at all.

(g) Lindblom objects to the synoptic view because it assumes that a single decision-maker can somehow appreciate all the information relevant to his policy problem which his specialist experts have provided—a point also made by Hammond *et al.* (1983). This is certainly a serious problem in the present case since the experts are asked to provide information on a vast number of topics, and from a whole range of specialties. Just how is this collection supposed to be put together to answer the policy problems now pressing concerning the control of lead in the environment? Whether or not a single decision-maker is required for a synoptic view to be achieved, it is clear that experts, with their partial view of the problem, must not be selective in passing information to policymakers. A rejection of information as irrelevant runs the risk that it may prove to be relevant when linked with other items from another group of experts. The NRC report points out that the US Federal Government sponsors research relating to the control of environmental lead which is undertaken by at least twenty-one agencies. To this may be added academic and industrial research which might be relevant. The collation of the efforts of all these diverse groups without overlooking what might be vital items of information is a daunting task. If all information garnered by the various groups of experts, each working on their own narrow research problems, needs to be passed into the decision-making machine, it can obviously only be in a highly compressed form. Policymakers are not equipped, and do not have time, for reading undigested reports of the findings of experts. Whatever the policymakers' own training, they are bound to be deficient in a number of the disciplines from which they are drawing expert advice. There therefore arises the familiar problem of compressing technical findings without distorting them. Of how this is to be achieved, the NRC report tells us nothing. It says nothing about the relationship between the suppliers and users of all the research they wish to be undertaken—the authors seem quite oblivious of the very great problems here.

(h) Together with the need for a synoptic view goes the need for centralized policymaking. Agencies with their special interests can only ever hope to achieve a partial view; what is called for is a single body to deal with lead which can achieve a genuine overview of the problem. The NRC report is therefore critical of the fragmented nature of present control in the United States, and proposes that agencies should work much more closely together than hitherto, perhaps with the formation of a better co-ordinating body, and perhaps with the establishment of a central agency to handle the problem of environmental lead. Lindblom is critical of such centralization on a number of counts: with a number of agencies involved any aspect of the problem overlooked by one is likely to be picked up by another agency. We should feel confident with the control of environmental lead falling to one central agency alone only if we could be sure that it had truly achieved a synoptic view of the problem and had overlooked nothing. We shall consider some examples of this later, in the next chapter. Even deeper than this is the need for specialized agencies and groups of experts to develop their own distinctive approach on technical matters relevant to controlling lead, so that the approach of any one agency may be challenged. We shall also consider examples of this later. A single agency would always be in danger of developing a complacent attitude towards those interpretations of the evidence which it favoured. In playing down the importance of the interpretation of scientific findings, the NRC report overlooks this crucial point.

(i) The results of the research outlined by the NRC only have value if they can be used for making decisions about the control of lead hazards; serious problems arise here, however. The report notes (p. 16):

> although it often makes the decisionmaker uncomfortable to attempt to quantify intangible values, every decision implicitly reflects them. The Committee believes that, where possible, it is essential to acknowledge and attempt to quantify values explicitly, and where this is less feasible, to recognize none the less that additional intangible values have been considered.

Lindblom objects to this call on the grounds that explicit statements of value promote friction between agencies. As the NRC report observes, an explicit statement of the reasoning behind an agency's decision may be corrected if others find it to be faulty, but against this, such scrupulousness promotes friction and delaying and costly controversy with rival agencies (p. 232). This is particularly so where values are concerned. The problem is that if, in making out its case, one agency employs a particular value which is not shared by another agency, there is the danger of a head-on clash of values which may prevent any decision at all being made. Collingridge (1982) has shown that agencies faced with this danger have a number of debating devices which switch the conflict from one about values, which threatens to be intractable, to one about facts, which can be settled in a straightforward way. Arguments between agencies about values should be avoided, and are avoidable by strategies of this kind. The express statement of values by agencies controlling lead therefore represents a distinct danger.

The NRC model assumes that risk-benefit and/or cost-benefit analysis may be applied to choose between alternative controls on lead. This not only poses severe technical problems, such as those associated with assigning monetary values to changes in health, but any application of such methods raises evaluative issues. This is particularly so when different income groups are affected differently by a proposed control measure. The problem usually presents itself in the form of how to compare benefits to one income group with costs assigned to a different income group. Lowering lead levels in petrol, for example, imposes costs on a relatively wealthy group—motorists—and confers benefits on a poorer group— inner city pre-school children (in particular). Comparing costs and benefits to different groups in this way involves the value judgement that the present income distribution in the society in question is the best possible one. Without such a value judgement, costs and benefits are not comparable, as the well-known failure of the Kaldor–Hicks–Scitovsky criterion shows. A fuller discussion is provided in Collingridge (1982). This makes any choice of control over lead hazards which the NRC would commend as rational dependent on the making of this value judgement. Other value judgements about income distribution are perfectly consistent and defensible, but they have the drawback of making cost-benefit calculations across income groups impossible. The NRC's decision model can only be used if this value judgement is adopted. The enormous effort to meet the research priorities identified by the NRC can only be used to control environmental lead if policy-makers are agreed on this value judgement; if other judge-ments about what is the best income distribution are made, this research is wasted. We would surely feel happier with a list of research priorities which was more robust than this.

Mixed Scanning

The full-blown type of synoptic rationality championed by the NRC is obviously no more than a dream in the face of the criti-cism mounted above, but there are weaker versions of the thesis which might be more successful—the mixed scanning approaches of Etzioni (1967, 1968), Gershuny (1978) and Dror (1964). It will be argued, however, that these suffer from many of the same problems. Etzioni accepts Lindblom's criti-cism of the synoptic ideal, but rejects disjointed incremental-ism on the grounds that it gives too great a weight to the powerful in policymaking, that many decisions are not in-cremental, and that it encourages bureaucratic inertia. Etzioni seeks a compromise position by adding two features to disjointed incrementalism. First, policymaking bodies are to concern themselves not just with everyday operational details, but are also to devote some of their energy to scanning the environment, both near and distant, for issues which might demand attention. Second, Etzioni distinguishes between fundamental and incremental decisions. The former set the direction for a series of incremental decisions, whose value and function is determined by the fundamental decision. For fundamental decisions, incrementalism is inadequate. The policymaker ought to consider all the main alternatives for such choices, trying to eliminate those options which reveal crippling objections. Not all options need to be considered in the same depth, for as soon such as an objection is found, the option need receive no further attention. The implementation of a fundamental decision is to be flexible and serial, and scanning should search for those problems caused by its implementation.

However, closer inspection with the help of the present case study shows that Etzioni's suggestions do not really provide a satisfactory theory of policymaking. Scanning adds nothing to disjointed incrementalism. Lindblom observes that scanning, in the sense of searching the environment for features which might imply change in an organization, cannot be conducted efficiently by the organization alone. Organizations have a vested interest in what happens in their environment and so tend to perceive events in a way which does not embarrass them. Correction is therefore likely to come from other agencies with other interests, who can argue that a particular change has occurred in the environment, and can pressure the first organization to respond to this change. Efficient scanning therefore calls for policymaking to be fragmented in just the way Lindblom advocates. It is also promoted if policy has a remedial focus, organizations searching the environment for features which they seek to avoid, and is serial, the search being continuous. But, again, these are features of disjointed incrementalism, features which ensure that this kind of policymaking involves efficient scanning in Etzioni's sense. No additional prescriptions are required.

The second novelty suggested by Etzioni—the distinction

between fundamental and incremental—collapses in the same way. Etzioni assumes that fundamental decisions cannot, and should not, be incremental. Decisions are nested in a familiar way. A firm's decision to lower the level of lead in the petrol it sells may follow from a decision to make higher levels illegal, and this in turn may follow from decisions to improve the environment generally and to set up the necessary apparatus. We may therefore think in terms of decisions which are 'relatively' fundamental. It does not follow, however, that these are not, or should not be, incremental. The decision to reduce the maximum level of lead permitted in petrol will later be shown to have been taken quite incrementally, and yet it is 'fundamental' to the many decisions of petrol suppliers to lower their lead levels. The existence of relatively fundamental decisions does not mean that they need to be separated out for special attention in a way which makes them non-incremental. It may be, of course, that relatively fundamental decisions require more thought and analysis, but this everyday observation can hardly be inconsistent with disjointed incrementalism. All that Etzioni can now realistically claim is that some relatively fundamental decisions should be made in a non-incremental way.

The final criticism of mixed scanning concerns the way in which the supposed non-incremental decisions should be taken. As Camhis (1979) observes, Etzioni assumes that policymakers have predictive powers which they do not possess in reality. To eliminate options in making a fundamental decision, less needs to be known about each option than is called for by synoptic rationality, which seeks to find the best option; nevertheless, a great deal needs to be known if an option is to be eliminated—more than it is reasonable to demand. To take an example: consider the fundamental decision over what approach to use in reducing the amount of lead in the air. One option in the United States was the adjustment of refining practices to produce a lead-free petrol of the same octane rating as before, so that no serious engine modifications were required. It was argued that this might actually cause worse health problems than those caused by lead in petrol through the emission of greater amounts of polycyclic aromatic hydrocarbons, some of which are suspected of causing cancer. This might be seen as a success for scanning the environment for problems needing attention, but what is noteworthy is the degree of uncertainty here and the great effort and time required to reduce it. The health effects of these chemicals are still largely unknown, and the dangers of emissions cannot be calculated, even after many years of research. This should come as no surprise after the earlier discussions, but it shows that mixed scanning runs into the same problems about technical information as the synoptic ideal does.

For fundamental decisions, all 'main alternatives' need to be considered. Etzioni urges this as a counter to the inertia of organizations, which he supposes to be encouraged by disjointed incrementalism. But options involving more than an incremental change soon begin to require large quantities of technical information. Etzioni seems oblivious of these problems and the embarrassment they would cause to policymaking if his proposals were adopted.

Conclusions

To summarize the arguments in this chapter: Lindblom's criticisms of synoptic rationality are cogent when applied to the control of environmental lead; the most serious problems arise from the sheer quantity of technical information which is demanded. It is clear that decisions about real world problems with a significant level of uncertainty cannot be made according to the ideal of synoptic rationality, nor according to anything approximating to it. Mixed scanning collapses into disjointed incrementalism when it is realized that the latter already provides machinery for effective scanning, and that the distinction between fundamental and incremental choices is relative. What is more, the way in which fundamental decisions are supposed to be made generates the same problems about technical information as does the synoptic ideal. An assessment of the ability of incrementalism to cope any better than its rivals must await the next chapter.

7 Lead—Realities of Policymaking

The Need for Compromise

Science is not the handmaiden of policy depicted in traditional mythology; none of the conditions for the efficient operation of science can be met when its results are supposed to be relevant to a political choice. It may now be asked how policy about lead should be made in the light of the limited use which can be made of scientific results, and the answer to this question may then be compared to how policy in this area was actually conducted. So far, the discussion has been negative, we have been concerned with what science cannot do, and with dispelling the illusions still fostered by the supporters of synoptic rationality—that science can be highly influential in the conduct of political affairs. The time is now ripe for a positive account of policymaking about lead. The key point is that whatever decision is finally made, and however it is arrived at, the option should be insensitive to any scientific conjectures. Put another way, whatever conjectures are used in selecting the final option ought to have a low error cost; their rejection should call for only the most modest changes in policy. This is an inevitable consequence of the now standard view of science, which sees its assertions as guesses open to criticism or negotiation. How policy can be made with this property is the issue for the present chapter.

As Brooks (1984), Hammond *et al.* (1983) and Rein (1976) point out, it seems to be a part of human nature for actors with an interest in policy to overstate their case, tending to highlight whatever bits of evidence support their favoured option and attacking those which threaten to undermine it—an effect clearly revealed in the present case study. Charged with the duty of protecting the environment and needing a significant bureaucratic victory, the Environmental Protection Agency interpreted the evidence available on the health effects of lead in petrol as showing that lead harmed children—just as the Ethyl Corporation defended the contrary interpretation. Not wishing to increase the political pressure for action against lead, the experts chosen to serve on the British Government's Lawther Committee interpreted the evidence on lead as indicating no need for special action, except at local hot spots—an interpretation contradicted by the Conservation Society who regard the problem as so severe as to require immediate and drastic action. What room is there for rational choice of policies for the control of lead given that such widely different views may be taken of the technical evidence? Throwing a coin to choose an option is a way of settling matters which has the advantage of simplicity, though little else: it offers no way of avoiding policy options which are sensitive to scientific conjectures. Should the coin favour removing lead from petrol immediately, this would be a tacit acceptance of the interpretation of the data supported by EPA, or the Conservation Society, and the option therefore remains highly sensitive to this interpretation. Whatever way the coin falls, the favoured option will be highly sensitive to some scientific conjectures, which is exactly what is to be avoided.

The bias held by actors in the policy process towards seeing evidence in a way which accords with their favoured options means that their assessment of the uncertainties surrounding the choices being made must be distorted. It is possible to interpret the evidence in a number of ways, but the single actor fixes attention on those aspects of the evidence which fit his interests, blinding himself to other interpretations by such devices as attacking the status of his critics and their technical advisers. Over-confidence in one's own views is the price of suppressing rival ideas, and it ensures a distorted evaluation of the uncertainties surrounding the issues being decided. A necessary condition for good policymaking, however, is a proper appreciation of these uncertainties. The Environmental Protection Agency's bureaucratic interests prevented it from making a realistic assessment of the uncertainties surrounding the toxic nature of lead, although this was in fact needed for good decision-making. A single actor will therefore make bad decisions—bad according to the actor's own interests and standards. Had the selection of policy for lead fallen to the Environmental Protection Agency alone, for example, the Agency might well have acted against many sources of the metal with great haste, paying no attention to the complaints of those bearing the costs, and this could have provoked a severe backlash against the Agency, leaving it in a worse position than before. Or else the easy implementation of policy against lead might have left the Agency with little need to support its bureaucratic position with another campaign against another pollutant which might, in fact, be more harmful than lead.

Good policymaking calls for many actors, each offering and defending their own particular interpretation of the available evidence. Each actor overstates the technical case for the option which is favoured, but finds that the option cannot be implemented because of the opposition from the other actors involved. Policy is eventually made by compromise between the interested parties. Compromise does not require any conversion on the part of the actors; they may well continue to be convinced that their technical case is vastly superior to that of their rivals who are not infrequently accused of using political force where rational argument has failed. An important feature of options selected through compromise is that they are very insensitive to any technical conjectures. Consider a simple case where just two actors are involved: an environmental agency A, and the industry B, although the case is easily generalized to many actors. A favours the complete and immediate removal of lead from petrol—option a—which is supported by an elaborate technical case. Likewise, B favours option b: no change in the amount of lead added to petrol. After some time the two agree on the compromise option, c, reducing lead levels to half of the existing ones over a five-year period. The compromise reduces the benefits that each actor perceives will follow from the favoured option. Believing that lead is poisonous, A has obviously lost benefits because the compromise will leave some people whose health deteriorates from lead in petrol. B's belief that lead is safe makes B see the cost of the compromise as the expense of halving lead levels in fuel, which cost falls to him. In compensation, however, the error costs which would be incurred by the actors are also reduced. If A is wrong, and lead is safe after all, option a would place severe error costs on B who would have to pay for the complete removal of lead. The compromise, c, obviously reduces these error costs, for B now has to pay to halve present levels of lead. Similarly, if B is wrong and lead is, after all, toxic, then B's favoured option of doing nothing would impose great error costs on the population which A is supposed to protect, and hence on A. Again, the compromise reduces these error costs since lead emissions are to be halved. Choosing a or b by tossing a coin offers the actors great benefits at the risk of great error costs, making whatever option is chosen highly sensitive to the technical case supporting it. Compromise, on the other hand, reduces the benefits to both parties, but offers compensation in the form of lower error costs. But lower error costs mean that the compromise option c is less sensitive to the scientific conjectures which A and B use in their technical debate. Compromise is therefore one way of ensuring the desired result, that policy be insensitive to scientific conjectures.

The need for a multiplicity of actors in the decision-making process is, of course, a central feature of incrementalist ideas of policy, as championed by Braybrooke and Lindblom (1963) and Lindblom (1965, 1968, 1979). Partisan mutual adjustment is the process by which actors, or partisans, seek to protect their own interests where these conflict with the interests of other actors—compromise through negotiation and exchange of technical information being of particular importance (Collingridge, 1982). The whole process provides a way of co-ordinating the policies of many actors without the need for the type of control where one actor stands above the rest, as insisted upon by the defenders of synoptic rationality. Partisans make choices by disjointed incrementalism—Lindblom's answer to the failure of synoptic rationality. With this view, partisans select policies by considering only a few options, slightly differing from the status quo, looking at only a few of the major consequences of each. The ranking of alternatives will depend upon their marginal differences, and it is on this restricted area that the efforts of policymakers and their advisers are concentrated. Analysis and evaluation are remedial, serial and fragmented. This view of how policymaking ought to be conducted and is conducted shares two features of great importance with the present account: there ought to be a plurality of decision-makers involved in policy, as mentioned above, and policymaking ought to make little demand on science. The incrementalist account of policymaking will therefore be considered with reference to British policy concerning lead, drawing on Collingridge and Douglas (1984).

Policymaking in Britain on Lead

(a)   *Policy is Remedial and Serial*

First, it is clear that all controls which have been placed on hazards from lead in Britain are remedial. In almost every case a remedy has been adopted for a recognized hazard to health. The extent to which hazards have been foreseen and avoided by undertaking radical moves to safer technologies is marginal. Even where dangers were seen as likely, the general pattern has been for the future to be left to look after itself. Once the danger has been identified, action is taken to remedy it; avoiding action is altogether far rarer. A good example here is lead in petrol, which has been added since the early 1920s. Early fears concerned those who were occupationally exposed, such as garage attendants and traffic police, and lead concentrations were limited to 0.84g/l. Calculations showed that increases in lead levels in the air and in dust from the then modest consumption of petrol would be marginal, so the ordinary public were not thought to be at risk. There was no attempt to predict petrol consumption twenty, thirty or forty years into the future, nor to foresee what scientific advances over the same time-scale might give indicators about more subtle injury from lead emissions. This is hardly surprising since no forecasting techniques could have provided estimates of miles travelled in the future, or of future knowledge of subtle health effects of sufficient certainty to have justified controlling lead in petrol more strenuously at the time. The future not being predictable, it was sensible for the decision-makers of the 1920s to leave it to its own devices. As the quantity of lead emitted into the air from this source grew, and as scientists began to explore the possibility of sub-clinical damage from lead, the time eventually came when action was thought to be justified. Maximum levels of lead in petrol in

Britain were gradually reduced to 0.64g/l from the end of 1972 to the present limit of 0.15g/l and will eventually reach zero.

The time-scale of this change illustrates a second feature of Lindblom's disjointed incrementalism—namely, the persistence of problems and the serial nature of their solutions. Of course, removing all lead from petrol would make an end, once and for all, of the lead-in-petrol problem, but even so the problem would have had a very respectable history, going right back to the early 1920s with fears about occupational exposure. The serial reduction in permitted lead levels in petrol is also characteristic. As limits have been lowered, the refining industry has had to make adjustments to provide a petrol which existing vehicles can use. This calls for considerable planning, and for some construction of new plant, which takes time. The serial solution was intended to ease the burden of this adjustment for the refiners.

The same points could be made with reference to lead piping in houses. Lead piping was installed between forty and a hundred years ago. It was known that under extreme conditions water could dissolve sufficient lead to cause clinical poisoning and even death, but in ordinary circumstances the pick-up of lead from piping seemed slight. Most hard water soon coated the pipe with a protective layer and, in any case, tended to precipitate lead. Some dissolution occurred with soft, acidic water, but the analytical techniques of the day could not measure the concentration of lead in such water. In the absence of reported cases of clinical poisoning from drinking domestic water, it was assumed to be safe to send water along lead pipes. When the pipes were being installed it was impossible to predict what lead levels in domestic water would be revealed by advances in analytical methods, and equally impossible to predict what sub-clinical effects of the metal would be found in the future. The pipes were installed and problems were left for the future. The first large survey of lead in domestic water was carried out by the Department of the Environment (1977a) and even this gives an incomplete picture because of the wide variation in lead concentrations which occurs in many domestic water supplies over time. In the survey, 4.3 per cent of households in Britain were found to have water with a daytime lead concentration in excess of the

World Health Organization's recommended $100\mu g/1$. With our present knowledge of lead hazards, these figures reveal a problem which demands a remedy. The point to be stressed is that those who laid down the piping could not have foreseen that this problem would occur so many years later on. If we attempt to blame them for our present troubles, then no one is free from blame, because no one can foresee the consequences of actions so far ahead; and yet decisions must be made.

The solution to the problem of lead in water is serial. Two approaches are being taken: the treatment of water which is particularly prone to dissolve lead, and the removal of lead piping from homes. The latter is, of course, a final answer, but it will take many years to complete the operation nationally, during which time water treatment may be used as a temporary measure, as discussed in Department of Health and Social Security (1980). The story is the same as that of lead in petrol: a crash programme of pipe replacement would be very expensive, requiring the training of an army of plumbers who would then be made redundant once the job was finished. If this is to be avoided and the building industry is to complete the job at the normal rate of working, with the normal number of plumbers, etc., then several years will be needed to complete the programme.

(b)   *Only a Few Options are Considered*

It is difficult for an outside observer of the policy process to know what options have been considered, if only because 'consideration' can cover a spectrum from brainstorming by junior civil servants in their coffee-break to publication of a White Paper. For present purposes reference will be made exclusively to literature which has been published by the relevant agency. Many more options than those discussed in print must have been considered, but at least we can be sure that those which have been published have been taken seriously. In the case of lead in domestic water, the only other option to have been considered in this sense is the coating of old pipes, but this has had little success. A further point, then, is that a restricted number of options were considered, all of which marginally differed from the status quo. Radical solutions to the problem of lead in water—such as the provision of standpipes, or of bottled, lead-free water, or of providing each household with a hydrogen supply and condenser—were simply not considered. Options are assessed according to the difference which they make to the status quo, otherwise the problem gets out of hand. The same is true of lead in petrol, where the only options considered were lowering lead levels in petrol and fitting filters to the exhausts of petrol-engined vehicles (Hansard 1978a, C.427).

Radical solutions, such as a massive shift from motor car transport in cities to diesel-powered public transport, were not considered. Comparing options which make marginal changes is relatively easy provided that attention is only paid to the immediate consequences. Moving from a lead limit of 0.84g/l to one of 0.64g/l, for example, brings such and such a reduction in air lead levels at such a cost to the motorist and refiner and adds so much to the balance of payments deficit, and these figures can be compared with the consequences of changing to other limits. But the attempt to assess something like a shift to public transport opens up more questions than can be dealt with at once. For example, will people resist such attempts? Should people who have invested in a motor car be compensated because they will only be allowed to use it occasionally? Will enough diesel oil be available in time, and with what changes in the refineries? What should be done with all the surplus petrol provided by the refineries? What will trebling or quadrupling the capacity of urban rail networks cost? How quickly, and at what cost, can a crash programme of training bus and train drivers be undertaken? And so on, and so on.

It should come as no surprise, therefore, to find that, in lowering lead intake from food in the population, the only ways which have been considered are those requiring marginal changes in agricultural practices (such as substitution of a new pesticide for a lead-based one) or food processing (such as reduction in splashing of lead solder in the manufacture of cans). Options such as compelling canners to use aluminium cans or cans with shorter seams to solder have not received serious attention, although such cans are in fact being developed. Edwards (1980) reports that these cans will be welcomed if they prove to be practicable and economic, but that legislating for their manufacture will do little to accelerate their introduction because of the great technical problems associated with their use for foods.

(c) *Policy is Fragmented*

According to Lindblom's partisan mutual adjustment, policy-making is fragmented, each decision-making unit concentrating on that part of the whole problem which it understands best and which is closest to its particular interest. According to Edwards (1980), thirteen government departments in Britain have had recent parliamentary questions asked of them concerning some aspect of lead. The Department of Industry, for example, is interested in occupational exposure and lead in paint, while problems of lead residues from pesticides fall to the Ministry of Agriculture, Fisheries and Food (MAFF). Government bodies such as the Health and Safety Executive and the Royal Commission on Environmental Pollution also have an interest in lead hazards, as do local government environmental health departments. At the other extreme international bodies such as the Common Market and the World Health Organization have an interest in the subject. Then there are industries at the receiving end of lead regulations which often have industrial research laboratories researching into lead hazards and the likely effects of pending legislation on the industry. Other research is carried out in universities and polytechnics, and pressure groups such as Friends of the Earth, the Campaign Against Lead in Petrol and the Conservation Society play an important part in the formation of policy.

The co-ordination of all this diverse activity, beyond a very rough-and-ready level, is simply not possible, for no one can achieve an overview of such dimensions. The truth of the matter is that each agency undertakes work on a narrow front because this is the only part of the whole problem which it can understand. Generally, an agency has a particular skill which it applies to the lead problem; no agency has the brief of examining the entire problem. A good example here is the work of MAFF on food standards. MAFF lays down food standards, and has achieved a great deal of experience and expertise in this. Most of these standards concern the description of foods and serve to protect the buyer from exploitation. Thus, for example, any food called 'strawberry jam' must contain above a certain proportion of that fruit. It is not illegal to sell food with less strawberries in it; it merely cannot be called strawberry jam. The imposition of such regulations requires considerable consultation with the industry and is rarely urgent. When the first lead in food regulations were formulated they fell to MAFF to implement, who employed the same machinery as for strawberry jam, although the problem was not one of cost, but of health, and so unusually urgent. MAFF held its normal consultations with the food industry, and the regulations took fifteen years to finalize. When these were reviewed the whole process was repeated, taking seven years. But this delay is the price paid for employing a system of food standards which is known to work. Setting up a special agency with its own machinery would probably have taken even longer, and would have risked passing regulations which were either unenforceable or unrealistic.

Problems neglected by one agency may often be identified and explored by another agency; this justifies each concentrating on its own narrow aspect of the entire problem. To develop an example mentioned briefly in Chapter 3, early research on the health effects of lead centred on those who were occupationally exposed. The industrial hygienist Kehoe, at the Kettering Institute in the United States, funded by the lead industry, did much of the early research on the behaviour of lead in the human body, a great part of which could not be repeated at other laboratories at the time. Kehoe's concern with occupational exposure meant that he only researched men, and men of working age who were fit. Kehoe's enormous influence on the direction of research meant that little attention was paid to children, women, old men, the foetus and people with various diseases. This is clearly seen in the famous controversy over Kehoe's $80\mu g/100ml$ blood lead threshold limit. Kehoe stated that, in his wealth of experience, no person had shown signs of clinical lead poisoning from an exposure which had produced a blood lead concentration of less than $80\mu g/100ml$, so that this could be viewed as a threshold limit, below which safety was guaranteed. Kehoe's experience, however, was with healthy, active men under medical supervision, as all lead workers are—and moreover, men who remain in a population screened for unusual sensitivity to lead. If a new worker shows signs of poisoning or if his blood lead level becomes unexpectedly high, he is moved from the job to one where he will receive a lower exposure to the metal. In this way the remaining workers are hypo-sensitive to lead. Nothing which could be said about this group could be said about the general population, which includes males who would be filtered out if they worked with lead, sick men, old men, women and children. But such was Kehoe's standing in the scientific community and so dominant was his work that his threshold limit was taken as applying to the whole population, which was then taken to be totally safe from toxic effects of lead (Collingridge, 1980, Chap. 12).

Nevertheless, attention was finally given to groups who had been excluded by this concern for occupational exposure. Naturally enough, this attention did not come from the industrial laboratories of occupational hygienists, but from research in various universities and medical schools which began to point to the possibility of sub-clinical damage in children. It is through this work that the $80\mu g/100ml$ limit for lead in blood across the entire population has been recognized as far too high, and as insensitive to differences across the population (Department of Health and Social Security, 1980). EEC regulations (Commission of the European Communities, 1977) call for the screening of the population for blood lead, and 'reference' levels state that 98 per cent of the population should have a blood lead level of $35\mu g/100ml$ or below. Any individual found to have a higher blood lead level must be investigated, and a search made for the source of excessive exposure.

(d) *Conflicts are Resolved in* ad hoc *Ways*

A second feature of the fragmented nature of policymaking is that conflicts between agencies tend to be resolved in an *ad hoc* way, not by some third party taking an overview of the problem which is causing the conflict. Conflict between the Department of Health and Social Security (DHSS), which, regardless of financial constraints, would have liked lead removed from petrol altogether, and the Treasury, which wished to see as little money spent as possible, was resolved by deciding to lower lead levels in petrol so that the total quantity emitted into the atmosphere should not exceed the amount emitted in 1971. With increasing mileage, this meant a steady reduction in the limit, as observed before. There was no attempt to perform the impossible task of a cost-benefit examination of reducing lead levels in petrol to see what the truly optimum level would be. This would require much more knowledge about the health effects of lead than is now available, and would be a very lengthy process (and hence costly). Instead, the cost of making a decision was reduced by a compromise. This can explain many curiosities about limits. For example, Waldron and Stöfen (1974) observe that the lead in food regulations allow a greater level of the metal in canned food than in the same item when it is fresh, and ask 'what can be the justification for allowing tinned foods to contain more lead than fresh foods?' This is indeed a puzzle if these limits are seen as devices to ensure the health of the consumer. If good health requires abstaining from eating sardines from a can with more than a certain lead content, then the same prohibition must apply to sardines fresh from the fishmonger. In fact, however, the lead regulations do not ensure that any food which meets them poses no health hazard. This simply cannot be stated, given our present limited knowledge of the health effects of lead, and our lack of detailed knowledge of the population's diet. Instead, the regulations represent a compromise between eliminating lead from food altogether, favoured by MAFF, and doing nothing, favoured in this case by the canning industry.

Right from the beginning, these standards have been designed, in the words of the Metallic Contamination Sub-Committee on Lead (1951, pp. 3–7) to 'limit the amounts [of lead] in food and beverages to the smallest quantities which are commercially practicable at the present time'. What is 'commercially practicable', of course, is a matter of negotiation between the parties concerned. To take another instance, this time from the Ministry of Agriculture, Fisheries and Food (1975), 'Levels are reduced as a result of natural factors and of changes in manufacturing techniques, and if statutory levels are set too low it may result in certain foods disappearing from the market because they may not legally be sold'. The same is true of limits on lead in petrol as revealed in Hansard (1978b, C589–90), and Department of the Environment (1976, 1977b). Compromises of this kind are, of course, very much less demanding of expert advice than the calculation of optimal pollution levels. Thus, setting environmental standards using Lindblom's disjointed incrementalism is a far less daunting task than could be imagined by any upholder of the synoptic view.

Another feature of policymaking on environmental lead which can be explained is the lack of co-ordination in the setting of standards. There is some attempt to co-ordinate research, and to parcel out various aspects of the problem to appropriate government departments, but the full co-ordination of policy is a task too daunting to be attempted. When limits on a particular source of the metal are discussed, no attention is paid to the way in which exposure from other sources might vary. For example, the lead in food regulations were revised in 1978, and many limits were then lowered. But between the first regulations and these amendments, the quantity of lead added to petrol had been reduced, and was to be reduced further still. No account was taken of this in formulating the amendments. If the aim had been to optimize the amount of lead in food, then recent reductions in air lead exposure would have had to have been considered. This consideration, however, would have demanded a vast quantity of data on the distribution of exposure from food, drink and petrol across the entire population. In the absence of such data, and bearing in mind the cost and length of time needed for their collection, a sensible strategy is for each source of exposure to be limited in a rough and ready and quite unco-ordinated way, which is exactly what is found to happen in practice.

The case study also enables an assessment of the major criticisms of incrementalism to be made. These are threefold: that decisions exist to which it cannot apply; that decisions go to the parties with greatest power; and that it encourages bureaucratic inertia. The first misses the mark altogether. Lindblom has never claimed that disjointed incrementalism can or ought to be applied to all decisions. Decisions to do wholly new things, such as going to war or setting up NASA, can hardly be made in this way, as discussed by Schulman (1975), Boulding (1964), Dror (1964), Self (1974) and Wiseman (1978). What would make the point tell is the existence of a class of decisions to which disjointed incrementalism could not apply, but which could be made effectively by one of the rival models. There are, of course, such classes; elementary games can be played according to synoptic rationality, but no more serious candidates have been suggested, and the present case study can find nothing which would serve this purpose, despite the attempts of Gershuny (1978) in this direction. Such a test has been undertaken in Collingridge (1984a), using the example of nuclear power, but the author comes down heavily in support of partisan mutual adjustment.

The case study also casts some doubt on the second criticism, at least if it is taken generally. The fragmentation which is essential for disjointed incrementalism ensures that power is diffused, and policymaking open, with agencies able to ensure that their opinions are heeded by a range of tactics, such as forming coalitions with other agencies. The injustice of this criticism can best be seen by considering the various limits which have been imposed on lead in petrol and in food and beverages. Here we saw that the limit is a political compromise between controller and controlled; there is no evidence from our case study to show that this is a rare occurrence.

The final criticism also fails to hold. Disjointed incrementalism is accused of encouraging the inertia which afflicts all bureaucracies, but the case study shows at least two bureaucratic innovations which counter this. These are the establishment of the US Environmental Protection Agency, which has had so much to do with controlling lead, and, in Britain, the use of the Food Regulations to limit lead in food and drink. In the first case, a wholly new apparatus was devised, which has proved to be very effective in controlling lead in the environment, and, in the second case, an existing bureaucracy was used for quite novel purposes. These innovations are not without problems: the EPA might be accused of being overzealous in its early days—as reflected in its debate with the Ethyl Corporation—and the use of the Food Regulations was a slow method of imposing controls. Nevertheless, they do show that disjointed incrementalism is compatible with considerable innovation in solving problems.

Conclusions of the Lead Case Study

It is now possible to draw the threads together and to arrive at some conclusions about the whole of the discussion on lead in this and the preceding two chapters. The first point, to which the whole of Chapter 5 was devoted, is that the technical debate about the health effects of low levels of lead fits the over-critical model very well. Loss of autonomy, interdisciplinarity and a rise in critical intensity all combine to prevent consensus on any issue which might be relevant to the formulation of policy for the control of lead in the environment.

This immediately raises questions about how policy is to be conducted in the absence of a technical consensus. The inability of scientists to reach agreement is the final nail in the coffin of synoptic rationality and some of its less extreme derivations, if one is needed, since making policy in the way enjoined by these approaches makes enormous demands upon technical information—an argument elaborated on in Chapter 6. The present chapter considers a more hopeful line of thought about the conduct of policy and incrementalism, particularly in the form of partisan mutual adjustment and disjointed incrementalism. These enabled an account to be given of how policy ought to be made in cases like the present where there is no technical consensus. Policy should be the outcome of adjustments by many actors—among whom power is fairly evenly shared—each able to defend his own interests by making out an interpretation of the available technical evidence which suits them. Each actor overstates his favoured technical case, but is corrected in this by the need to compromise with other actors who hold different views of the evidence. Policy is produced by compromise between these actors, and as such it is highly insensitive to scientific conjectures, much less so than if policy were the creation of a single, all-powerful decision-maker. This view of policy was not only able to offer prescriptions for political choice in the absence of technical consensus, but also gave a good description of the actual policy process concerning the control of lead in Britain.

The case study has also helped us unknot the myths about policymaking and about science which are so closely interwoven. Synoptic rationality demands that policy be formulated by a single decision-maker, or by a well-defined group, blessed with the time, resources and political space which allow for a full overview of the problem in hand, along the lines envisaged by the National Research Council's report on lead discussed in the previous chapter. Policymaking in this way demands an enormous input from science—only possible given the mythological view of science described in Chapter 2 which sees nothing but satisfaction in the marriage of science and policy. The myths of rationality and of the power of science come together in this story of how information from science can be employed in making political decisions. For all its attractions, the story cannot hold together. In reality decisions are made in the *ad hoc*, 'seat of the pants' ways described by incrementalism. Most decisions, as Weiss (1982) recognizes, are not made, but merely happen, brought about by the changing circumstances and fortunes of the political actors who are involved. Weiss and Bucuvalas (1980) describe how difficult it is to find anyone bold enough to confess to being a decision-maker in the sense required by synoptic rationality, each actor playing a very marginal, and often unrecognized, part in the policy process through interaction with other groups of actors. To talk of decision-makers—or worse, of *the* decision-maker—is to prefer myth to reality.

Synoptic rationality makes quite unrealistic demands on science, especially in cases like the lead issue which exemplify the over-critical model. The real function of scientific research in a case like lead is in ironic contrast to the bold role of mythology. Far from science being a natural handmaiden to policy, the efforts of scientists in the lead debate are to provide counters to the claims of other scientists, the technical case for one policy option being balanced by that supporting a rival option. The scientist's task, in co-operation with those who wish to use his results in their political struggles, is to unwittingly overstate the technical case for one option, so that the overstatement of the technical case for the rival option does not go unchallenged. The policy which finally emerges is a compromise which relies hardly at all on the detailed work of technical experts. Nevertheless, scientific research has an important, if lowly, place in policymaking, for rivalry between expert groups is an essential antidote to the selective deafness which seems to be a part of being human. Without technical debate, one group of experts would dominate the policy process and choices would be made with a very distorted conception of the uncertainties which are involved—a recipe for poor decision-making.

The aim of this book is to undermine the twin myths of rationality and the power of science. The literature on incrementalism is now very considerable and the poverty of synoptic rationality and its derivatives have been much discussed. In what follows, therefore, emphasis is given to the more novel ammunition against the myth of the power of science provided by the over-critical model. From now on, our concern will be more with science than with policy.

8 IQ in America—
The Over-critical Model

A second example of the over-critical model will be described in this chapter—the debate about the inheritance of intelligence. Theories of intelligence have received very different treatment in America and Britain. Hot debate has been associated with these ideas in America since their earliest formulation in the first years of the present century, while the same theories managed to dominate British psychology without a word of dissent until at least 1945. Chapter 8 will therefore look at the American debate, in particular at how closely it fits the over-critical model, with the following chapter considering the British story. Theories of intelligence provide a good example for present purposes because they have always claimed to be highly relevant to matters of policy, although the discussion here will concentrate on educational policy only.

Throughout most of the present century psychology in Britain and the United States has borne the ever-present theme of the existence of general levels of mental ability—intelligence—which is largely inherited and therefore difficult or even impossible to improve through well-intentioned social policies and education. At times, these ideas are totally dominant within psychology, only to fade a little later, but remaining always in the background, waiting for the resurgence which changing conditions and fashions inevitably seem to bring. These ideas have not remained walled up in the laboratories of experimental psychologists, however; on the contrary, they have always been intimately related to politics, where their influence appears, at least, to have been a substantial triumph: at last a social science strong enough to be relied upon in matters of policy. Tests based on these theories of intelligence have been used to select army recruits, to choose immigrants of suitable quality, to select pupils and students for schools and colleges, in the streaming (tracking, in the United States) of students, in their selection for various career opportunities, and after that, promotion within their organization. Generations of citizens have been guided through education and later life by these tests in both countries, but particularly in America.

Development of such social technologies does not, however, exhaust the influence of theories of intelligence on society. Of far greater significance than any specially designed test, no matter how useful, is the picture of society which the psychologists paint, a picture with profound implications for all political actors. It is a society where differences in wealth and social position are to be explained by differences in the innate mental capacities inherited from one's parents. Social distinctions may no longer be thought of as injustices, they are merely reflections of the differing degrees of efficiency with which people can find their way in society. Those whose mental capacities are limited by their genetic make-up, much as they may struggle, can never hope to match the achievements of their rivals with superior parentage in the struggle for social status and wealth. The inheritance of social position is no longer an injustice perpetrated by the powerful on the weak; it is the result of the transmission of genes for intelligence across the generations. Middle-class children spend longer at school, become better qualified and earn more money in occupations of high social standing, but the envy of the working class is quite misplaced for such are the rewards for the intellectually able. Attempts to alter the status quo, to improve the abilities, education, job prospects and earnings of the working class are essentially misplaced, most of the difference between the two groups being determined by their different genetic constitution which, of all things, is the most unchangeable.

Early intelligence tests in America were used to identify children with special needs, but routine testing of all pupils became standard practice from the 1920s, the results being used as an aid to streaming (tracking). By 1932 about three-quarters of city schools used intelligence tests in this way. The year 1947 saw the setting-up of the Educational Testing Service (ETS) whose expenditure grew from an original $2 million to $30 million by 1969, when it was described by Karrier (1972) as 'the doorway to virtually every profession

in the corporate liberal state'. Criticism has always surrounded testing in America, though varying considerably in
intensity. The defenders of the tests described their role as
the efficient allocation of educational and career opportunities across the population, arguing that judgements of
such importance should not be left to the subjective opinions
of teachers and employers who are likely to be biased against
many minority groups in society. The tests' opponents argued
against them on many levels, some holding that minor altera-
tions to test scores were needed in fairness to women, men,
blacks, working-class children or whoever, others rejecting
outright the whole concept of IQ as a measure of intelligence.
Since IQ is supposed to be largely inherited, these debates
became entangled with even more wide-ranging arguments
about the relative roles of nature and of nurture in human
development.

An early attack on IQ testing was made by the famous jour-
nalist Walter Lippmann (1922–3) which stimulated a brief but
furious debate. In the early 1950s and 1960s the heat of criticism increased markedly as educational reform became the
vehicle for wider social change in the struggles over civil rights
and the poverty programme. Tracking in schools which
employed IQ tests placed a disproportionately high number of
black pupils in low tracks—an offence which became increasingly challenged. For some twenty years the ideas of inherited
IQ and of the racial inferiority of blacks lay dormant, only to
be revitalized in the 1970s by the psychologist Jensen (1969)
who appealed to traditional theories to explain the failure of so
many of the optimistic environmental programmes of the
1960s. They failed, Jensen suggested, because of the inherited
limitations reflected by a low IQ.

These arguments over IQ testing are very reminiscent of
those over the effects of lead on health. In both cases masses of
data accumulated over decades of research, and yet the technical issues remain as unilluminated as before, or worse, the
darkness deepens as the debate brings into question more
issues than it resolves. Despite all the research and all the findings, wholly divergent views can still be maintained: that lead is
harmful, that lead is harmless; that IQ is a meaningful measure
of intelligence, that IQ testing is a pseudo-science. Lippmann's

case against IQ testing in 1922 was based on the following points:

1. The normal distribution of IQ is not an empirical discovery of psychology but a convention imposed on IQ scores.
2. Tests need to be standardized, and this is often done with small, atypical groups.
3. Test items are completely *ad hoc* in the absence of any theory which can guide test constructors.
4. Even if IQ measures intelligence, it is a measure of a very narrow set of intellectual skills.
5. The correlation between IQ and teachers' assessment of pupils is disappointingly low.
6. IQ test scores may be influenced by many extraneous factors such as the emotional state of the child.
7. IQ testing detracts attention from the weaker children whose poor performance can be put down to their genetic limitations, over which teachers have no control.
8. IQ scores correlate with social status, thus social position, not IQ, can explain the distribution of wealth, achievement and educational attainment.

This happened in 1923. In 1953 exactly the same case was made out against IQ tests in Britain by Simon (1953). Jensen (1980, 1981a) gives a lengthy defence of IQ testing which has had to go over exactly the same ground; he defends himself from criticisms which could have been made by Lippmann himself. Sixty years of debate have hardly advanced the argument—there is still as much disagreement over the use of IQ testing as there ever was; no major contentious issue has been thrashed to consensus. Remember that we are talking not of the political acceptability of IQ testing, for political rows can happily go on for sixty generations, but of the technical debate about the theoretical justification for IQ testing.

The science of psychology certainly looks a little sick. The hypothesis to be defended in this chapter is that the technical debate about IQ testing is an example of the over-critical model. Science flourishes where its practitioners are autonomous workers in well-defined disciplines in an atmosphere of limited criticism. These conditions are met neither in the lead debate, nor in the debate which is our present topic. The failure of these conditions means that poor quality work is done, that disciplinary confusions obscure argument and that the level of criticism increases as those engaged in the argument recognize the political consequences that the technical debate might have. People wish to be highly critical and criticism is particularly easy because of the poor quality of work and the interdisciplinary confusion with which it is beset. Under such conditions, there is no hope of scientific research promoting a technical consensus. Whatever results are reported are subject to radically different interpretations and the technical debate becomes to all intents and purposes unending. This pattern is to be found in all aspects of the American IQ debate, but a complete coverage of it is hardly possible within our present compass. Instead, we shall concentrate on one episode in the story—the debate sparked by Jensen's 1969 article—and pay particular attention to those aspects of the Jensen debate which shed light on our thesis.

The curtain was raised by the publication in 1969 in a very obscure journal of an article by the psychologist Arthur Jensen with the provocative title, 'How much can we boost IQ and scholastic achievement?' Two claims in the paper in particular were to spark off years of stormy debate, though they were hardly new, having been out of fashion since the early 1950s. IQ was held to be strongly linked to one's heredity, to about 80 per cent or so, and the hypothesis put forward was that the familiar and persistent underscoring in IQ tests by blacks was due to genetic differences also supposed to be inherited to about the same degree. The message was the old one again: compensatory education had failed because of the inherent limitations of the human material to which it had been applied. The abilities, and hence educational attainment, of individuals is severely limited by their genetic make-up, and one cannot hope for improvement from environmental changes such as those attempted in the compensatory programmes such as Headstart. In particular, the lower IQ of blacks, who figure so prominently in compensatory programmes, appears to be largely genetic.

What follows is an analysis of the debate which Jensen's article generated, although no claim to completeness is made.

Particular attention is paid to those troublesome features found in the lead debate—loss of autonomy, interdisciplinarity and an increased degree of criticism.

Loss of Autonomy

Research on the effects of lead on health was found to be of poor quality because scientists had addressed problems posed to them by policymakers. This is true of the present study also, only more so, for educational psychology is a discipline which has as its very foundation the promise of delivering understanding which is relevant to practical questions of teaching and the organization of education. To enter the discipline, researchers must forgo their customary freedom to explore whatever seems to them of theoretical interest and promise; the problems they are to explore are, at least in part, defined by those outside the discipline. They have therefore chosen to work on perhaps the most intractable species. Human beings have an enormously complex nervous system, making for interactions with the environment of extreme complexity, to which may be added their long lifespan—all of which combine to make humans very unsatisfactory subjects for scientific research. Add to this the impossibility of experiment, and psychology begins to appear all but an impossibility except for the very brave. The situation worsens when psychology explores the nature/nurture interaction in human beings. This is hard enough for properties determined by a single gene, but is far more complicated with properties such as intelligence where many, perhaps thousands, are involved. Studying this kind of inheritance is difficult enough with properties such as height where data is hardly open to question, but when intelligence is explored the problems are compounded by the means by which it may be measured. IQ theorists have therefore taken on research of a quite extraordinary difficulty. It is hardly surprising to find that the results they regard as established can be made to look very shaky in more critical hands.

Much of the educational psychologists' laboratory is, of necessity, to be found in the outside world where lucky accidents produce situations which come as close to the ideal as the harsh world allows. A key piece of evidence in the inheritance of IQ is provided by identical (monozygotic, or MZ) twins separated at birth and brought up in very different environments. These twins have grown from a single egg which divided after fertilization, giving them identical genes. Whatever features separated twins share are therefore likely to be largely determined genetically (colour of eyes, for example), whatever striking differences there are (e.g. hairstyle) being the result of their environments. Jensen (1969) restates the standard case for an IQ largely fixed genetically; his estimate is 80 per cent, in which separated identical twin studies play a central part. He reports no new findings, merely providing an overview of evidence found in any standard textbook.

It is interesting to compare the separated twin studies done in the real world, in less than perfect conditions, with an ideal study. Three conditions are necessary for an ideal study: the twins sampled must be genetically representative of the population at large; the twins must be reared in environments which are representative of those found across the whole population; and there must be no tendency for the environments of the twins to be systematically correlated. These might be achieved by gathering twins from a sufficiently wide number of families to satisfy the first condition, and separating them at birth at random, to satisfy the third condition, taking care to meet the remaining condition by taking a sample of babies across a sufficiently wide range of environments.

Returning to the real world, the first problem is the great scarcity of separated identical twins, which places a severe restriction on the quality of conclusions which can be drawn—other problems apart. There are only four such studies, the largest of which, by Cyril Burt, is now discredited as fraudulent. Kamin (1974), supplemented by Taylor (1980), examines the three remaining studies in great detail. He identifies many failings, the most important one, and that of most interest to us at the moment, being failure to meet the third condition for sampling. In other words, the environments of the twins were far more similar than randomly chosen environments, which greatly inflates the importance of genes in determining IQ. The typical pattern is of twins separated soon after birth, one being kept by the natural mother, the other by a close relative or nearby friend of the family. Many attended the same school, and went on shared family holidays and outings. Some were separated after a number of years together, others were reunited after a period of separation, giving them a common environment for part of their lives.

The painful reality of experimenting in the harsh world outside the laboratory is nicely illustrated by the Chicago study of Newman *et al.* (1937) who looked at nineteen pairs of identical twins. To save travelling expenses, the researchers were keen to exclude non-identical twins, which they did by confining themselves to twins who thought themselves extremely alike. This saved money, but it biased their sample against identical twins who were physically, and perhaps mentally, quite different. A further saving made was to exclude twins living very far apart, but this too biased the sample by excluding twins reared in widely differing environments. To help obtain enough volunteers, the twins were promised a free trip round the Chicago fair. In the midst of the Depression, how many twins exaggerated the differences in their upbringing for such an epic treat?

Such are the perils of experiment in the real world. In the necessary compromise in such research between the demands of the ideal case and the messy realities of life, it is not surprising that research results are open to widely different interpretations. For Jensen (1973), 'the overall intraclass correlation of ... 0.824 ... may be interpreted as an upperbound estimate of the heritability of IQ in the English, Danish and North American Caucasian populations sampled in these studies'. But in the view of Kamin (1974), 'to the degree that the case for a genetic influence on IQ scores rests on the celebrated studies of separated twins, we can justifiably conclude that there is no evidence to reject the hypothesis that IQ is simply not heritable'. The fight goes on, however, with Jensen (1975a) restating his earlier conclusion, only modified in the elimination of Burt's work, and Kamin in turn has restated and developed his criticisms of the twin studies in Eysenck and Kamin (1981). Taylor (1980) accepts Kamin's objections to twin studies which he extends to the work of

Jencks *et al.* (1972). Jencks re-analysed earlier data on IQ to obtain a correlation of 0.81 between identical twins. Taylor's recalculation using less risky assumptions gives a correlation which is less than that between the IQs of non-identical twins. One can only sympathize with the remark of the psychologist, Scarr (1981, p. 4):

Intelligence is a very complex phenotype with a very complex developmental sequence. For those reasons it is not an ideal phenotype for behaviour-genetic analysis. The importance of human intellect in human affairs is so great, however, that an abdication of the pursuit is not excusable either.

As in the case of lead, animal studies are far easier to perform, but their relevance to human intelligence is even more doubtful.

Interdisciplinary Problems

A clear source of confusion, misunderstanding and frank error in the research directed towards an understanding of the health effects of lead is its interdisciplinary nature. This is found in an equally striking way in the IQ debate where the disciplines of psychology, genetics and sociology overlap in the attempt to understand intelligence. Harwood (1976, 1977) tries to explain why individual scientists took up the position they did, pointing to disciplinary influences as well as ones external to science. Our interest, however, is more with the content of the debate.

(a) *Psychology and Genetics*

Educational psychology traditionally takes a fairly straightforward, no-nonsense view of inheritance. If a property of an organism, such as IQ in humans, is largely determined by the genes an individual is born with, then there is little room for change by way of altering the organism's environment. If genes give a person blue eyes, then blue eyes they will be, more or less whatever environmental changes occur. Moreover, whatever environmental changes may be found to alter the inherited property, all individuals will be affected in the same way. In particular, since IQ is largely inherited, attempts to raise the

IQs of a group of children by a particular educational experiment are likely to raise all the individual scores by about the same amount. This view of inheritance clearly lay behind the support given by psychological theory to sterilization laws and immigrant quotas. Immigrants from Eastern Europe were banned from the United States not because of their low IQ scores, but because this defect was likely to be passed on to generations of sub-standard offspring, even allowing for the very different environments of the United States and the immigrants' home countries. The low IQ of these people's offspring would not be appreciably changed by whatever social conditions could be offered in America. The theory of IQ inheritance was popular with teachers for the same reason: a child's poor performance is not a reflection on the school's failure to provide the right environment, but a result of the inherent limitations of the pupil to respond to whatever environment is offered.

The traditional concept of inheritance surfaces in many places in Jensen (1969), for example in his discussion of the decline in national IQ which includes the warning that 'current welfare policies, unaided by eugenic foresight, could lead to the genetic enslavement of a substantial segment of our population' (p. 178 in the 1972 reprint), and in his discussion of the inheritance of mental retardation (p. 175). In a passage soon to receive much criticism, Jensen suggests that since IQ is more strongly inherited than scholasic achievement, there are more ways of changing teaching patterns to increase achievement than to raise IQ scores (p. 135). Indeed, the central thesis of Jensen's paper, his explanation for the failure of environmental programmes to raise IQ or school performance, depends crucially upon this traditional concept of inheritance. If IQ is strongly inherited, it is to be expected that it would be resistant to change by the environment. This, however, is not a view of inheritance which is shared by geneticists. They see the interactions between genes and the environment to give the final properties of an individual organism as being extraordinarily complex. Figure 3 shows how the height of a plant might vary with temperature, all other environmental factors being constant, for three different genetic constitutions of the plant, or genotypes, G_1, G_2 and G_3. The graph for each is characterized by a threshold below which there is no growth, and by a steadily increasing slope after that until a plateau is reached. The differences in height at any particular temperature are entirely genetic in origin, while the differences in height of one genotype grown at different temperatures are entirely environmental. But to say that G_1 is genetically taller than G_2 at temperature T_2 says nothing about what happens at different temperatures. At T_1, for example, G_1 is genetically shorter than G_2. The example is highly simplified, of course, but it straightaway reveals the old nature/nurture divide, 'how much of a plant's height is determined by its genes?' to be a pseudo-problem. In reality, of course, a property such as height depends upon hundreds of environmental factors which themselves interact in far from simple ways. Growing G_1, G_2 and G_3 in varying nitrate concentrations may alter the temperature/height relationships in Figure 3 and may do so in a very non-uniform way.

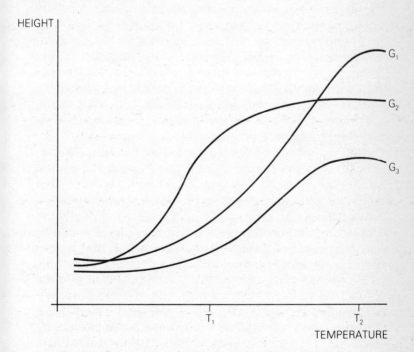

Figure 3 *Variation in height with temperature of plants of three genotypes*

Jensen borrows a term from genetics, 'heritability', in order to express the results of twin and other studies of IQ. The heritability of a property in a population is the proportion of the property's variation (technically measured by its variance) which derives from variations in the population's genes. Jensen is at pains to make all the reservations about the use of heritability which it is customary for geneticists to make. He warns, for example, about taking strong heritability to entail immutability (pp. 119–20). The genetic defect of metabolism associated with phenylketonuria has a 100 per cent heritability—those with the gene will contract the disease and none of those possessing normal genes will ever develop the disease, no matter what kind of environment they may find themselves in. But, for all this, the disease is treatable. If an early diagnosis is made, the sufferer can lead a nearly normal life by adjusting his/her environment very slightly to avoid various foods (p. 120). Heritability also changes when a population's genes alter or when the environments to which the individuals in the population are exposed change. Jensen gives the example of susceptibility to tuberculosis. When everyone was exposed to the bacteria causing the disease, the differences found in their response, some becoming infected quickly, others resisting disease, were due to differences in genes and therefore of high heritability. When exposure to the bacteria became rare, differences in infection were mostly explained by the luck people had in avoiding contact with the bacteria, which is therefore of low heritability (p. 120).

There is therefore a distinct tension in Jensen's case about the heritability of IQ. If the modern genetic notion of heritability is accepted, it seems that the high heritability of IQ says nothing about how environmental changes can alter IQ in the population, nor about the heritability of IQ once some of these environmental changes have been made, ruling out any explanation for the poor performance of educational programmes.

The tension was immediately exploited by several geneticists: Dobzhansky (1973), Lewontin (1970, 1974, 1976), Hirsch (1971), Gottesman (1968), Layzer (1972, 1974), Block and Dworkin (1974), Cancro (1971), Morton (1972), Medawar (1977) and Thoday (1969, 1973), who object to Jensen's interpretation of the 80 per cent heritability of IQ, if not to the measurement of heritability itself. They remind Jensen of the limitations on heritability, which he is formally aware of, but which he does not seem to have taken to heart. The full development of this point requires a few technicalities. Jensen's (1969) calculations of the heritability of IQ depend on some important simplifications. The first of these is the condition of additivity, according to which the genetic and environmental influences on a trait in a population add up in a straightforward way. If additivity held for weights, then giving everyone an extra food intake, say 300 cals/day, would increase the weight of all individuals by the same amount, regardless of their genetic variation. In this case, the effect of environment and of genes on weight gain can clearly be isolated and treated separately. The second condition, that of independence, holds that environmental and genetic variations are not related. In the case of IQ it is easy to see how this condition might be broken: those individuals with the genes for a high IQ may be more selective of environments which enhance their own IQ than their counterparts who are less blessed by inheritance—a tendency which would utterly confound attempts to attribute such a degree of IQ to genes and such a degree to environment. The geneticists' criticism in technical terms is that for such a complex feature as human intelligence the two conditions needed for a simple estimate of heritability cannot conceivably be met, making talk of heritability, let alone its measurement, altogether meaningless.

In his defence, Jensen (1973, pp. 50–4) argues that additivity for IQ should be assumed on grounds of simplicity, as is customary in animal breeding trials, and he also appeals to the analysis of Jinks and Fulker (1970) who failed to detect any significant interaction between genes and environment for IQ which would have shown additivity to have broken down. In turn, Taylor (1980, pp. 159–60) is very critical of Jinks and Fulker's methodology which he accused of making an assumption of what is to be tested. Having defended his measurement of heritability of IQ, Jensen (1973) goes on to restate the policy implications of this estimate. In selecting farm animals for their high milk yields or their egg production, if the trait in question has a strong heritability, then breeding will be the best approach. If heritability is poor, experiments with environment will be needed, and both approaches might be useful together for the intermediate case. The strong heritability of IQ with today's distribution of genes in the population and the current distribution of environments means that a redistribution of teaching environments across pupils will not have much effect on IQ, although there is always the possibility that wholly new educational environments may change IQs dramatically.

The debate about heritability has reached no consensus and the first convert is yet to be made. It clearly indicates the presence of the same interdisciplinary confusions and misunderstandings that we found playing such a prominent part in the analogous debate about the effects of low levels of lead on health. Standing back from the tangle of technicalities which can so easily obscure the picture, it can be said that the psychologists approached the problem of the heritability of IQ in quite a different way than the geneticists. For the psychologists, remembering that Jensen stands at the end of a very long tradition of such analysis, the problem is to relate two features of relevance to their subject. Relating IQ to the genetic composition of the population is, for them, the same kind of puzzle as relating IQ to social status, or to income, or relating smoking habits to nailbiting. The tools for all these studies are provided by the analysis of variance which seeks to explain the variation in one property in a population by means of the variation in another property. Such studies might reveal that 20 per cent of the variation in the population's smoking habits is explained by differences in the way they bite their nails; that 15 per cent of social status can be explained by IQ; or that 80 per cent of IQ can be explained by genetic contribution. Conducting such analyses obviously calls for some simplifications, but a hard line against simplifying difficult problems would destroy scientific progress. The geneticists bring quite a different vision. They appreciate the tremendous complexities of the way genes and environment can interact in such a sophisticated organism as man, viewing in horror any attempt to impose the absurdly improbable simplifications needed before the analysis of variance can be used on subtle properties such as intelligence. This clash of disciplinary insights is at the root of the protracted and bitter debate we have outlined here. Similar confusions surround arguments about Jensen's claim that the differences between IQ scores in the American Black and White populations may be genetic in origin; but the reader may be spared the technicalities.

(b) *Psychology and Sociology*

A radical challenge to the orthodox interpretation of IQ is offered by a group of sociologists, and prominent among these are Bowles and Gintis (1976) and Karrier (1972). They deny that the real function of mental testing is the promotion of social efficiency by enabling the education offered to children to be moulded to their individual talents and limitations. Instead, they say, the real purpose of testing is one of social control—the preservation of existing inequalities in wealth and power. IQ tests are designed to favour middle-class children over their poorer social rivals, the very test items themselves revealing a manifest reflection of middle-class values, opinions and tastes, often relying on the kind of exposure to literature and verbal skills fostered in middle-class families. The use of mental tests in selection for scarce educational resources ensures that the children of middle-class parents are better educated, better qualified, and earning more, in jobs of higher social status than their working-class rivals. The correlations between IQ and educational attainment, earnings and social position which give credence to mental testing are not the result of the middle classes having better genes for IQ; it is in fact a deliberate discrimination against the working class and the Blacks who make up a disproportionate part of this group in America. All mechanisms of social control run into the problem of how to prevent resistance from the controlled. Legitimation is provided by the army of professional psychologists bearing the message that low achievement, poor jobs, inadequate education and poverty are basically due to limited intellectual apparatus, largely determined by genes and therefore resistant to improvement by the normal processes of education.

There appears to be very little room for argument between the psychologists such as Eysenck, Herrnstein and Jensen and the radical sociologists. These psychologists had to employ various concepts from genetics in talking of the inheritance of IQ, with all the confusions and arguments which this predictably generated, but in the present case the two disciplines, psychology and sociology, have no need to borrow in this way. There is, therefore, very little ground upon which the battle can be waged. There seems to be only one empirical finding which is relevant to the argument. Bowles and Gintis (1976) argue in support of their radical analysis by pointing to the low partial correlation between IQ and income. IQ scores affect income in two ways: people with high scores will receive better education and hence higher earnings and people with high IQ scores ought to be better at their job, whatever it is, than those with low scores, and hence ought to earn more. But many studies have shown the second effect to be trifling. If the incomes of people with the same education are compared with IQ, there is only a small correlation. It follows that IQ does not affect work performance directly. It does so only indirectly, through the correlation between IQ and schooling. The psychologists' meritocratic hypothesis that those with high IQ earn more because they are better at their work is therefore falsified. What correlations exist between IQ and income are almost entirely the result of the correlation between IQ scores and schooling, itself a social artefact designed to perpetuate the favoured position of the middle class.

In reply, Jensen (1980, pp. 344–6) argues that there are thresholds of intelligence for jobs: anyone can be a potato peeler but all brain surgeons need an IQ of at least, say, 100. If the figures for the partial correlation of IQ with income were really as low as those quoted by Bowles and Gintis, anyone would be able to do any job, thresholds would not exist and every level of IQ would be found in every occupational group. Since this is not what is observed, the partial correlation is much higher, which is likely to be revealed when more sophisticated statistical devices are applied to the data. The reply is telling, in that it shows how little room there is for real engagement between the psychologists and the sociologists, since the relevance of the existence of thresholds of IQ to the debate is itself dependent on which side one is standing on. If access to jobs was completely open, unfettered by socially constructed impediments, the low partial correlation between IQ and income would indeed lead to people of all IQs doing all jobs. IQ would not be a significant determinant of employment and there would be no thresholds. Thus, the existence of thresholds shows that the partial correlation is higher than supposed by the radical critics, but only on the assumption of free competition for employment. For the sociologists, education artificially restricts the employment opportunities open to people: there is no free competition. IQ testing ensures that middle-class children receive higher qualifications, which give them access to more highly-paid jobs. The threshold is not one of IQ, but of qualifications. The thresholds that are observed for IQ in employment merely reflect the socially constructed correlation between IQ and qualifications. The existence of thresholds cannot be used to distinguish between the conventional and radical interpretation of IQ testing since both can provide a consistent explanation for it.

This appears to be generally true. Consider, for example, Jensen's (1980) argument against the radical interpretation, that a substantial fraction of the inequalities of social status within a family is related to differences in the IQ of its members. Those middle-class children lucky enough to have an IQ greater than their father's tend to have an even higher occupational status, and vice versa. This is compatible with the psychologists' view that IQ measures ability which determines social position, but unhappily it is equally consistent with the sociologists' hypothesis. Defence of the legitimacy of IQ testing requires that not all middle-class children receive their parents' privileges; this would make the whole exercise a little too transparent. If IQ is to exercise its social function, a few middle-class children with low IQs must be sacrificed, just as some working-class children with high IQs must be promoted—the change of status being largely brought about by the type of education to which the children are exposed on the basis of their scores.

This tells us a great deal about the problems of interdisciplinary research: where two disciplines offer rival explanations for a phenomenon which differ profoundly there may be no possibility of employing empirical evidence to further the debate since any item of data can receive a consistent interpretation from both disciplines. The sociologists and the psychologists in our present example are therefore condemned forever to talk past each other. There can be no empirical basis to their disagreements.

Rise in the Level of Criticism

It is clear that, after Jensen, the IQ debate operated at a very much higher level of criticism than is customary in pure science whose research results are of no relevance to policy. Jensen's (1972) preface describes the very stormy reception which his original article received. The following issue of *Harvard Educational Review* was taken up by critical articles, the *New York Times* report of the controversy generated a record number of letters to the editor and campus activists called for Jensen's dismissal. The Society for the Psychological Study of Social Issues (SPSSI), the Association of Black Psychologists and the American Anthropological Association launched critical attacks on Jensen's claims. Jensen (1972) contains a bibliography of articles sparked off by his 1969 article which, after only two and a half years, had 125 entries. The editors of *Nature* (1972) and the American National Academy of Sciences (cited by Vernon, 1979, p. 281) objected that although scientists were free to explore all issues, they must remain sensitive to the effects of their findings on the public. Much of the debate has been conducted in the strongest possible language, accusations of racism being hurled at Jensen and his colleagues and his theories being smeared by reports of its history which play up its earlier connection with some particularly unsavoury eugenics movements in America (Kamin, 1974). The reply includes worthy volumes (Jensen, 1980, 1981a) in which the author tries to explain his thesis with such striking clarity as to overcome the many 'obstacles to clear thinking about IQ'.

There are other features of the debate which show its difference from arguments in normal science; Jensen (1981b) contains a section where he condescends to provide the reader with his own views on the philosophy of science—a sure sign of some sort of crisis. Specific discussion is also found of the relationship between science and policy and the consequent degree of criticism which is appropriate. Eysenck and Jensen favour the traditional view: scientific results must stand irrespective of their relevance to policy (the principle of irrelevance); in particular the level of criticism applied by scientists should be quite unaltered by any social consequence which the claim in question may have, or be thought to have. Thus, Eysenck in Eysenck and Kamin (1981) criticizes Kamin for being far too critical of Jensen's theories. Science, Eysenck objects, is always full of minor anomalies which can all too easily be exaggerated out of all importance by an adversarial critic. Science can only operate when criticism is moderated and conducted in an atmosphere of the co-operative search for truth. Both Scarr (1981) and Jensen (1981b) complain that their papers receive far closer critical attention from editors and reviewers than those of their environmentalist opponents. In reply, the critics expressly dismiss the principle of irrelevance: Hyman (1969) and Kamin (1981) restate the position implicit in the *Nature* editorial and the National Academy of Sciences' statement that hypotheses like Jensen's which may have dire social consequences if in error, should be subject to much closer scrutiny than normal; this is the only approach open to the socially responsible scientist—a view also taken by Ezrahi (1976) in commenting on the debate.

Endless Technical Debate

The arguments following Jensen's original article of 1969, of which we can give only a very partial coverage here, went on for a number of years and continue to this day. The history of the conflict is even more venerable, however, because of its part in the eighty-year-long debate about the influence of nature and nurture on human abilities. The post-Jensen debate resembles that surrounding the health effects of low levels of lead in many striking ways. First, the debate seems to be without end; it has an extraordinary resistance to the data which have been provided in abundance. As observed earlier, Lippmann's criticisms of IQ testing made in 1922 are still current, and contemporary psychologists are obliged to defend themselves against these ancient rebukes, despite the enormous quantity of data collected in the intervening decades. Second, a very wide range of opinions about IQ can be sustained even in the face of this data. It is not simply Jensen versus the anti-Jensenites, although this impression may have been given by the necessarily limited discussion given above. Jensen, Eysenck, Herrnstein and Shockley are contemporary representatives of a tradition dating back to the early part of the century, just as their opponents restate views of equal vintage. Despite all the data which has been so assiduously collected, it is possible, at one extreme, to assert the traditional psychological position that IQ is a genuine measure of intelligence, being largely fixed by genes. At the other end of the spectrum is the radical critique of the sociologists which sees testing as a method of social control operated by the powerful against the weak. In between these extremes virtually all possible positions seem to be filled. The psychologist Scarr (1981) disagrees with Jensen only in holding the heritability of IQ to be somewhat weaker and racial differences to be non-genetic. Vernon (1979), also a psychologist, finds it impossible to measure the contribution of heredity and environment in the present state of the evidence, although he hopes for continued research, while another psychologist, Taylor (1980), is much more sceptical, though holding that the heritability of IQ is likely to be above zero. Beyond them comes another psychologist, Kamin, who casts technical doubts on the whole concept of IQ and its measurement: a diversity of opinion no less worthy of comment than the spread of ideas about the toxic effects of environmental lead.

A third feature common to both debates is that as the position of each side becomes more articulated and as more evidence is accumulated, instead of at least some areas of disagreement being closed off, there is ever more to quarrel about. Far from approaching consensus, the debate opens up more and more issues. Lippmann's suggestion that IQ tests are constructed to favour middle-class children has been developed into the radical critique of Bowles and Gintis and Karrier who can now appeal to evidence in favour of their hypothesis—the low direct effect of IQ on earnings. Far from settling any questions about class bias in IQ testing, these have only succeeded in generating arguments about the reality of the low correlation which have all the features for a very long run. As the hereditarian analysis has been refined with the introduction (long before Jensen, as it happens, by the way) of measures for the heritability of IQ, it has resolved no contentious issues but instead opened up the battlefield of whether this concept is at all appropriate to IQ. Jensen (1973, pp. 117–9) and Eysenck (1971, 1973) tried to resolve issues of heredity by appealing to the empirically observed regression to the mean in IQ across generations— an effect they regard as only explicable on a genetic hypothesis. But nothing has been settled; rather, the measuring of regression to the mean has been added to the topics under discussion by, for example, Bodmer (1972), Kamin in Eysenck and Kamin (1981), Li (1971) and Vernon (1979). Whatever technical issues the debate touches upon seem to be drawn into it. Kamin (1981) recognizes as much when he denies the pleas from Scarr and Jensen for more empirical research, for, whatever its findings, they will be as open to multiple interpretation as all the earlier ones.

A final feature common to both the lead and the IQ debates is the practice of selective citation. With so many rival hypotheses and such oceans of data, it seems altogether unavoidable. If a 'fair' overview of scientific evidence is a theoretical possibility, it is certainly not possible for our IQ debate. A typical case is discussed by Layzer (1972). Jencks *et al.* (1972) estimate the hereditability of IQ separately for data of four different kinds, as shown below.

Heritability of IQ is between 29 and 76 per cent from parent–child data

45 and 60 per cent from twin data

29 and 50 per cent from identical twins reared apart

0.0 and 25 per cent from siblings and adopted children reared together

Layzer points out the large degree of room for interpretation in the light of preconceived notions which must exist with such an imposing spread of numbers. Jensen uses this data to put the heritability at 70 to 80 per cent; Jencks himself obtains a value of between 35 and 55 per cent. Jencks is more sympathetic than Jensen to the environmentalist thesis. Kamin (1981, p. 468) argues that 'the sheer quantity of the data collected makes selective reporting inevitable', and recites a case where unexpected failures to reveal a high heritability of IQ in two twin studies remained hidden in Ph.D. theses because by themselves they meant very little—although together they obviously have much greater influence.

Conclusions

The IQ debate can now be seen as a further example of the over-critical model. Conjectures as to the inheritance of intelligence and genetic racial differences in intelligence have important implications for policy, favouring policies which prove offensive to many people. These claims are therefore subject to much more critical scrutiny than is normal in pure science. If the hypotheses of Jensen and his fellow thinkers are adopted, they imply radical changes for education. If these changes are implemented and the hypotheses are, after all, proved false, then heavy error costs would have been incurred. The error cost associated with these conjectures is therefore far higher than the error cost of any pure science conjecture which has no implications for the real world. It is therefore perfectly rational to search for error in these cases far more strenuously than in pure science: a much higher level of criticism is appropriate. Work on IQ deals with a notoriously difficult experimental subject, *homo sapiens*, in the hope of discovering useful results, but this means that much of the research is of poor quality. To this may be added the problem of the interdisciplinary nature of the understanding of human behaviour which adds its own peculiar confusions, misunderstandings and failures of communication. Loss of autonomy and disciplinarity mean that it is particularly easy to criticize research findings and their interpretations in this area—a point exploited by those looking for criticism. As with the case of lead, in IQ research people wish to be far more critical than is appropriate to normal science, this being quite rational, and criticism is particularly easy. Thus, debate is endless.

Although the main purpose of this chapter is to test the application of the over-critical model to the technical debate over IQ in the United States, a few words are called for on the relevance of this large research effort for education policy, although a full discussion is best postponed to the end of the next chapter. The endless technical debate over lead prevents any scientific conjectures in that area from having any significant influence on policy, and the same may be expected here. American policy on education must be developed without a technical agreement on any issues relevant to IQ testing; policy must therefore be insensitive to the various conjectures which fight it out in the scientific debate. The defenders of testing would like to see its use in education extended, overstating the technical case which supports its use; reformers want to rid education of tests and similarly overstate the technical case against IQ testing. Whatever policy results from this political clash is best seen as a compromise between the groups involved. Being a compromise, policy is sure to be highly insensitive to all the claims made in the technical debate. The efforts of the scientists, for and against IQ testing, therefore have an ironical influence on policy. Such research is destined to have no direct influence on the way the world conducts its affairs; at best it has an indirect influence in that it tends to cancel out research results which favour the other side. Education cannot be built around the views of Jensen and his supporters, nor around those of Kamin and his camp, and yet without Kamin, Jensen's work might have had great influence, and vice versa. To put it in jargon: rivalry between research groups ensures that educational policy which is sensitive to the theories of any side is not made, leaving us with the happy result that policy in this area is insensitive to all scientific conjectures.

9 IQ in Britain—The Under-critical Model

Criticism Absent

The first intelligence tests in Britain were devised to help in the identification of pupils who required expensive remedial teaching. In 1919–20 trials were made in two areas, Bradford and Northumberland, investigating the possiblity of using group intelligence tests to select pupils for free secondary school places at 11 years of age. At this time schools were run by local education authorities, supervised by a national Board of Education. There were broadly two types of school, elementary schools taking children from 5 to 13 or 14 which charged no fees, and secondary schools which were fee-paying and selected children at 11. The latter schools were modelled on the public schools (private schools, in America), offering a heavily academic syllabus as against the more practical bias of the elementary schools. There was intense competition for the few free places—less than 5 per cent of the age group— (Morris, 1961), which secondary schools offered, paid for from local or central taxes, and it was this problem of selection which was posed to the rapidly expanding band of specialist psychologists.

The Bradford and Northumberland experiments stimulated interest on the part of the largest education authority, the London County Council, which was the first to employ an educational psychologist—none other than Cyril Burt. The year 1921 was a key one in the widespread introduction of testing, seeing the publication of the favourable report of the Northumberland study which in Sutherland's (1977, p. 145) words 'inaugurated group testing as an industry', and of Burt's handbook, *Mental and Scholastic Tests*. Shortly after, in 1924, the Report of the Board of Education's Consultative Committee on *Psychological Tests of Educable Capacity*, chaired by Haddow, gave support to IQ testing for selection for free secondary places. Several psychologists made important contributions to the report, the first chapter being written by Burt.

Intelligence is defined here by Burt as 'inborn, general, intellectual efficiency'. Details are then given of various tests, comparing the results of the new psychological test with the existing examinations for free-place scholarships and the opinions of teachers, which show good agreement. Burt then describes the 'remarkable achievement' of IQ testing in the Civil Service where the results of the test give the best correlation of all the tests taken with overall results. The Report observed that IQ tests give a good indication of children's innate educational capacity, are fairer to children than other tests, are easier to mark than existing examinations, provide an objective measure of intelligence against the subjective opinions of teachers, and have a built-in compensation for the age of the pupils being examined. The effectiveness of the new tests was defended by three types of evidence: comparison with teachers' opinions of their pupils, correlation with earlier tests and follow-up studies of children's school careers. The view taken of intelligence was a crudely genetic one, a child's inborn abilities placing a limit on what could usefully be taught.

The recommendations of the Report, which Sutherland (1981) describes as slowly taken up by the education authorities, were that IQ testing might be a valuable supplement to existing tests for free-place scholarships at secondary school, which should be examined experimentally by seeing how closely the results of the two were correlated. The new tests were unlikely to completely replace the old or to displace the judgement of teachers, but they could provide valuable supplementary information. New courses in experimental psychology and statistical methods were also recommended for teachers to be able to adminster the new tests and understand their significance.

The last recommendation highlights the developing relationship between psychologists and teachers and educational administrators which is so important in the understanding of this period of British educational history. The new but rapidly expanding discipline of psychology was eager to prove its usefulness to outsiders, just as outsiders were seeking new associations with science which might raise their professional status and fight off control by laymen. Early clients of pscyhology were psychiatric doctors, educationalists, teachers and personnel managers. In return for professional status, psychology received the benefits elaborated by Doyle (1979) and Sutherland and Sharp (1980). Experimental research could be done with the co-operation of clients, and its results published in the journals of the client: client demands for more training courses led to the establishment of new psychology departments and career opportunities appeared for psychologists within the structure of client professions. For educationalists, psychology represented a tool for the transformation of an occupation into a profession, providing the objectivity of science with which to fend off lay control. Once the training in experimental psychology and statistics recommended by the Consultative Committee's Report was widespread, teachers enjoyed greater authority in the conduct of their affairs. Educationalists pressed for the training of teachers in universities, the first course of this type beginning in 1905 and already covering many topics in psychology. Most teachers were still taught their skills in training colleges, but here too more and more attention was given to psychology from 1890 onwards and within this area mental testing was increasingly singled out for particular treatment. By the late 1920s psychology was widely regarded as the real basis of the education of teachers in the training colleges. In 1924 Burt was appointed Professor of Educational Psychology at the London Day Training College, as many lesser posts were steadily being filled by people with qualifications in psychology. Frisby (1969) estimates that by 1962 more than 60 per cent of training college staff were so qualified.

The relationship between psychologists and teachers was sealed when the educationalists' journal, *Forum of Education*, became the *British Journal of Educational Psychology* in 1930. Career prospects for psychologists opened within education with the employment of Burt in 1913 by the London County Council as the first professional educational psychologist. Mental testing became the chief research interest of educational psychologists in Britain, though by no means the only one. Blackwell (1943) shows that about 70 per cent of Ph.D. theses were concerned with mental development and capacity, of which three-quarters concerned intelligence testing.

Teachers welcomed educational psychology and did much to foster it, as we have seen. They were therefore quite uncritical towards the theories and techniques propounded by the psychologists. No criticism could be expected from teachers, and educational administrators, but what is more puzzling is the virtual complete absence of dissent from any other quarter until the early 1950s. Free-place selection restricted the education of many working-class children who could certainly have benefited from secondary education, so the absence of any criticism of intelligence testing on the part of the trade unions or the Labour Party needs some explanation. Throughout the whole period, from the beginning of this story until 1944, the chief political argument about education was the number of free places to be made available in secondary schools, after which came the raising of the school-leaving age, the type of schools which should cater for 11-plus education and what syllabuses they should follow. No attention was paid to the methods by which those few children were to be selected for scholarship places; debate focused entirely on the number of children who should receive the privilege. From the beginning of the century to the early 1950s there was no criticism of educational psychology or of its offspring, IQ testing. Throughout this whole period psychology in Britain developed in a curious isolation from the debates about nature/nurture which shook the United States at various times. As we have seen, there has been a constant technical debate in that country about IQ testing and the psychological theories which sustain it, although the intensity of argument has varied considerably, but nothing of this was imported into Britain, where educational psychology dominated thinking for half a century.

Here then is a puzzle: in the case of lead in the environment, the policy implications of the results of scientific research were challenged so dramatically that the debate over policy generated a matching technical debate about the metal's toxicity which promises to run forever. In the present case, however, the products of science, the psychologists' IQ tests, were applied in the making of educational choices with no significant challenge at all. Here then is a counter-example to this book's sceptical thesis that science has no relevance to policymaking. If scepticism is to prevail, it must be shown that, despite appearances, the work of psychologists had no influence upon the conduct of British educational policy. The first point to note is that during this period educational psychology was not seen as relevant to the major political issue in education—the number of free secondary school places that should be provided—and this is no accident. Unlike the case of the sciences entangled in the debate about lead, educational psychology grew up alongside teachers and administrators who looked to the new science for immediate assistance in their practical tasks. In order to break with its philosophical origins, British psychology consciously strove to serve communities beyond the laboratory—doctors, managers and teachers—by providing them with tools with which they could do a better job. As Hearnshaw observes (1964, p. 201), applications saved psychology. In particular, IQ tests were designed to aid teachers in selecting children for elevation to the ranks of the few free secondary school places. If educational psychology had to prove its usefulness to teachers, it would hardly risk challenging this crucially important client group. Research which might have been embarrassing for teachers and educational policymakers was avoided, just as useful research was encouraged. Nowhere did psychology argue that the teachers' problems were misconceived and in need of reformulation in the light of the latest research findings; rather, it offered technical tools for the smoother performance of the teachers' traditional tasks and a comforting theory about the limitations of pupils' abilities being due to their genes.

Educational psychologists not only managed to steer their research clear of any political controversy, but they did the same with other disciplines too. A notable feature of the debate over the effects of lead on health are the confusions which arise from the involvement of many scientific disciplines, but IQ testing in Britain, on the other hand, was introduced by educational psychologists alone, offering no challenges to members of other disciplines who might have seen an opportunity for a contribution of their own. Of the disciplines which might have fought educational psychology in this period, sociology had not really been invented (Hearnshaw, 1979,

p. 22), and social psychology was only a little more advanced, its division of the British Psychological Society only being set up in 1940. Developmental psychology was a much stronger candidate, but it had very close links with educational psychology, numerous contributions being made by Burt himself. With its concern for the mental and intellectual development of children, this area could have posed a threat, although it managed to live in harmony with psychometrics and factor analysis, with the same researchers contributing to both fields. These were, in fact, seen as complementary, developmental psychology being concerned with the ways in which the genetically limited intelligence of the child was applied and developed through education and experience. Thomson (1968) has also pointed out that, before 1950, the developmental psychologists were principally concerned with experimental problems rather than theory. Any clash with geneticists was to come many years into the future.

The success of educational psychology in avoiding conflict does not stop here, for there was very little disagreement within the confines of the discipline. Research in educational psychology was centred on University College, London where Spearman, and later Burt, held the chair, and was dominated by a handful of people of considerable influence within the expanding band of professional educational psychologists. Disputes were therefore confined to marginal issues. The other important centre of British research in psychology was Cambridge, although work there was dominated by experiment, with no party line on theory except for a dislike of statistics which meant that little criticism could be expected of the work of the London school (Crompton, 1978). Central concern within British psychology between the wars were McDougall's humic theory, psychoanalysis, and the factor approach to human intelligence of the London school. McDougall's theories, being based on the notion of purposive striving as the characteristic mark of behaviour, with instincts as the ultimate source of energy, offered no particular resistance to theories of intelligence. Indeed, as Hearnshaw (1964, p. 212) observes, they were seen as parts of a wider framework of a comprehensive account of personality in its dual aspects of conduct and ability. Nor was there any conflict between psychoanalysis, with its emphasis on therapy, and work on intelligence.

While in other countries psychology was fragmented into a number of disputatious schools, its development in Britain was free of such conflict. Behaviourism was never taken seriously enough to become of critical concern; with the origins of British psychology based in philosophy, behaviourism was almost defined out of existence for psychology was seen as the study of experience. The nature/nuture debate seemed to hold no more interest than behaviourism—indeed, the whole of British psychology was insulated from the debates so hotly pursued in America. The only point of contact between work in the two countries was a modest transfer of information within educational psychology. The Americans strongly objected to McDougall's theories, and the British showed no eagerness to take on the American involvement with problems of learning, the conditioned reflex, or experimental approaches to the study of personality and social psychology.

Educational psychology in Britain resisted any kind of debate, a point which is quite fundamental to understanding the relationship between this science and educational policy-making. Where policy was concerned, educational psychology offered no challenge to the current orthodoxies of teachers and administrators; instead it won their eager acceptance by confirming what they wanted to believe about children. Teachers, educationalists and policymakers were able to carry on more or less exactly as before, except that they had now acquired the armour of scientific professionals and a whole set of new jargon with which to keep it polished. But easy acceptance had a very severe cost for educational psychologists in Britain. Unable to challenge the status quo, the discipline could exercise no real influence on policy. It could be adapted to legitimate existing policies, but could play no part in changing them. Change can only come with those ideas which will challenge orthodoxy, but it is just this threat that was deliberately avoided by the psychologists. Educational policy would have been largely the same throughout this period if educational psychology had never been thought of, or had been confined to the seminar rooms of University College.

This claim will now be defended by looking at a number of cases where the ideas and instruments of educational psychology seem to have had an influence on policy.

(a) *Psychological Tests*

Psychologists found a ready market for their tests in the education system, where teachers and administrators had long felt the need for some sort of objective test, particularly for 11-plus selection for secondary schools. After the First World War political criticism of the existing scholarship examination began to grow as demand for secondary places continued to far outstrip supply. Most authorities operated a qualifying examination—all of those lucky enough to pass being eligible for secondary education—but many of the families of these children could not afford the financial burden entailed. In any case, most of the secondary school places were filled by fee payers who normally had no effective entrance test to pass. In 1919 the Board of Education recognised the problem, urging that all children should take a competitive test of capacity and promise rather than tests of attainment. The Board therefore concentrated its attention on the development of tests to determine children's educational capacity at the age of 11.

The principal plank of the case for IQ testing, heard time and time again from its proponents, is that its selection of children for secondary education is virtually the same as that made by earlier methods which relied on formal examinations and teachers' opinions. The new tests therefore brought no major changes in the selection process, their overt advantages being merely ease of administration, cheapness of marking, and so on. It is clear that educational psychology had no real influence on the policy of selection; it did not affect the choice of candidates for advantaged education, but merely the manner in which the choice was made. Had educational psychology never been thought of, very much the same children would have been selected in the competition for free secondary places.

(b) *Selection at 11-plus*

The same pattern is found in another aspect of policy to which educational psychologists had something to contribute—the age at which children should pass from primary to post-primary education. Psychological theory held that adolescence begins at 11 or 12 and that children of this age have varied interests and abilities—in the words of Board of Education (1926), making it 'possible and desirable to cater for them by means of schools of varying types, but which have, nevertheless, a broad common foundation'. But in proposing 11 years as the age for transition from one kind of education to another, the psychologists agreed with a practice and body of opinion which Kazamias (1966) traces back to the previous century. Since 1902, most examinations for free scholarship places at secondary schools had been given to pupils at age 11. From this time on, there seems to have been a complete consensus among teachers and administrators that, for state schools at least, 11 was the appropriate age for the end of primary education, as it has remained in Britain until today. The Consultative Committee to the Board of Education, again under Haddow, reviewed the whole question in its 1926 report, *The Education of the Adolescent*, finding teachers, psychologists and administrators all agreed on the importance of the 11-plus transition. The report upholds the consensus, stating that arguments from psychological theories are reinforced by practical considerations. However, the report's recommendations, its constant emphasis on the general agreement among teachers, administrators and legislators, and the long history of discussion and organizational development based on the age 11–12, suggest that this statement could well be reversed. Practical considerations and the long-established experience of teachers were reinforced by educational theory. As before, the theories developed within educational psychology did not challenge educational orthodoxy, they merely reinforced it. In doing so, it lost any hope of influencing educational policy. Without the work of educational psychologists, the transition from primary to post-primary education would still have continued to be made at 11-plus.

(c) *Varieties of Post-11 Schools*

Psychologists argued that the diversity of children's talents and interests after 11 becomes sufficient to merit separate schools for children beyond this age—joining the already wide consensus on this policy issue among teachers and administrators. Agreement continued, as we shall see, until the 1950s, when reformers began to support the introduction of comprehensive schools (then called multilateral schools) which would take in pupils at 11 from all ability groups. Rubinstein and Simon (1973) review earlier discussion about comprehensive schools, but the new schools were generally seen as being large buildings containing several sub-schools under one roof. Throughout the period of the present study, there was agreement on the need to provide different types of post-11 schools—it was merely the best means of achieving this that was being debated. In the much-quoted phrase of Tawney (1922), 'equality of educational provision is not identity of educational provision'. In this spirit of diversity grew up the higher grade schools, science schools and junior technical schools alongside the traditional secondary schools. Diversity suited both reformers and conservatives. Simon (1974) shows convincingly that the Board of Education wished to protect established secondary schools by encouraging other types of school which were administered differently, while the Labour Party saw these other schools as an opportunity to reform the traditionally narrow teaching offered by the secondary schools.

It is clear that the theories offered by educational psychology were appealed to in the debate about the variety of schools as a legitimation of a reality largely determined by the adminstrative needs of the existing system of post-11 education. Rubinstein and Simon (1973) claim that the report of the Consultative Committee of the Board of Education under Spens, in 1938, rejected comprehensive schools on grounds derived from psychology, but this is mistaken. The Committee's reasons were, in fact, all administrative ones: problems of size, the role of the sixth form, the difficulty of finding headteachers competent to run such broad-based schools, and the special needs of technical education. The highly influential Spens Report talked of different types of children requiring different types of school, but there was no basis for this in any current theory of educational psychology. The conclusion here is as before: without the blessings of educational psychology, the same types of school would still have existed.

(d) *Streaming*

The practice of streaming (tracking) was a response to pressing practical problems in the classroom rather than a result of any illumination shed by educational psychology. Primary schools began to promote gifted pupils likely to achieve a scholarship place in the early years of the century, and this generated problems of classes with children of widely differing ages, described in Burt (1917). By the early 1920s, this was being overcome in some schools by streaming, with three classes for the different abilities at each age level. Streaming then spread to post-11 schools and schools were encouraged to be sufficiently large to contain three or four parallel classes in each year group. As Simon (1974, p. 243) observes, once again the advice of educational psychologists corresponded exactly to the administrative pattern which was emerging. In 1925, for example, Burt recommended to the London County Council a treble-track system with classes for slow, normal and advanced pupils—a suggestion echoed by psychological advisers to the 1931 report of the Consultative Committee of the Board of Education (under Haddow again). With or without the opinions and researches of the educational psychologists, schools would in fact have been streamed in very much the same way.

It is clear from these examples that for the period 1900–45, the primary relevance of educational psychology to matters of educational policy was one of providing justification for existing policies. Without educational psychology, education in Britain would have functioned in the same way; the same children would have been allowed the benefits of free secondary places—though the methods of selection would have been different—streaming practices would have been unchanged, primary education would still have ended at 11 and there would still have been the same variety of post-11 schools. Educational psychology deliberately avoided questioning the orthodoxies of the time. The price paid for the easy acceptance which it won from this cowardice was the inability to influence policy. The interests of teachers and administrators were well served by the psychologists—no criticism could be expected from them—and the political attention of educational radicals was concentrated on the issues of the expansion of free places in secondary schools and eventual free places for all pupils able to benefit from such education. Here is the explanation of the technical consensus on educational psychology, particularly on the use of IQ tests, despite the raging disputes which erupted from time to time across the Atlantic. Educational psychology in Britain touched no live political issues and so enjoyed a happy isolation from the American debates about IQ testing and the wider issues of nature versus nurture. The next section continues the history and describes the collapse of the consensus in educational thinking.

Criticism Begins

After the Second World War British education was radically changed and the consensus of the early period began to collapse, with dire consequences for educational psychology. The Education Act of 1944 is still seen as one of the great liberal reforms of British society for it finally gave free secondary education to all children and raised the school-leaving age to 15—changes which had been delayed for decades by the Depression and the Second World War. The educational duties of local authorities were defined very broadly in the Act, no particular type of secondary schools being stipulated. The newly formed Ministry of Education was to supervise the education offered by local authorities which had to have their new development plans scrutinized. The Ministry was therefore able to strongly influence the pattern of schools, although there was no statutory model. The Ministry's favoured model was the tripartite system, where at 11-plus children were selected to join one of three secondary schools—now known as grammar, technical and secondary modern schools. As might be expected, these were based on existing schools, the old secondary schools becoming grammar schools, junior technical becoming technical schools and central becoming secondary modern schools. There were only a few technical schools, however, and in many areas the system was in fact bipartite.

Selection for schools at 11-plus was no longer influenced— or so it was argued by the income of parents, all places being free, but by examination of language and mathematical skills and by intelligence tests which made up the 11-plus examination. In a few areas, comprehensive schools were established, taking in children of all abilities who therefore had no need to take these tests, but the reorganization brought about by the 1944 Act greatly expanded the workload of the IQ testers. And here lay the seeds of their fall from grace. With the achievement of free secondary education for all and the raising of the school-leaving age, the reformers naturally enough looked to the next step—universal comprehensive schools. Income still influenced educational opportunities, for the children of middle-class parents stood a far better chance of obtaining a place in a grammar school than did their working-class peers. Equity demanded the final abolition of parents' ability to buy better education for their children through the abolition of the tripartite system in a place of comprehensive schools drawing in children of all classes and incomes. Early rumblings of this argument could be heard before the Second World War, but the argument began to gather momentum from the early 1950s onwards. This was bad news for educational psychology, which provided the rationale for the types of secondary schools and the methods of selecting pupils for them. Two other factors which Ford (1969) reports as helping to bring the 11-plus onto the political agenda were the postwar baby boom, which in the middle 1950s kept many middle-class children from receiving the grammar school education expected by their parents, and the growing success of secondary modern school pupils in gaining qualifications which showed that they had been wrongly placed by the 11-plus examination. Whatever the balance between these various factors, and whatever other social changes added to their momentum, by 1955 there was no hope of a return to the consensus of earlier days.

Early criticisms of the 11-plus test were administrative rather than technical, for example pointing to the huge differences in local grammar school provision—from 9 per cent of the age group to 60 per cent. Another point of contention was that IQ test scores could be inflated by coaching children and giving them practice papers, a practice not so damaging in itself, but seen as generating great unfairness, with some schools playing the 'gentlemen' and refusing to coach and others beating the system by regular coaching. Intelligence testing came under further technical attack from the Cambridge psychologists, Bartlett (1948), Chambers (1943), Heim (1954) and Zangwill (1950). Nothing in their arguments was particularly new, however, raising the question of why they had not been put forward years before. The answer is provided by the critics: they were concerned with the influence that theories of educational psychology were having on the promotion of unpopular educational policies. As the longstanding truce between British schools of psychology was eventually broken, arguments against testing began to be heard from researchers in related disciplines who had been silent until then. Social psychologists, represented by Blackburn (1945, 1947), stressed social influences on IQ scores. Geneticists also began to question the longstanding assumption of the educational psychologists, as in Penrose's (1950) attack on the psychologist Vernon (1950) at that year's British Association Meeting. Even more important were the arguments of educational sociologists such as Halsey and Gardner (1953) and Floud, Halsey and Martin (1956) who studied educational progress and social class. The early debates between psychologists and sociologists of education are reviewed in Thompson (1961). Criticisms of both kinds were developed in Brian Simon's widely read *Intelligence Testing and the Comprehensive School* (1953). As mentioned in the previous chapter, Simon's criticisms may have been novel to their British audience, but they were familiar to anyone with the least acquaintance with the American debates, from Lippmann (1922–3) onwards. These criticisms had been prevented from reaching the British consciousness by the consensus on policy between educationalists, teachers, administrators and psychologists, but the shifting sands of politics now gave them an audience eager for ammunition against the 11-plus selection.

The British psychologists had no Jensen; their retreat—indeed virtual collapse—was almost immediate. With criticism mounting, the British Psychological Society (BPS) published a review of the current state of the art under the chairmanship of Prof. Vernon (Vernon, 1957). It is admitted that the normal distribution of IQ in the population is an artefact imposed by psychologists on the raw data, although a stuttering defence of the assumptions involved is offered. Intelligence itself changes from 'inborn, all round intellectual ability' to 'more general qualities of comprehending, reasoning and judging, which have been picked up without much specific instruction . . . not . . . innate abilities'. The predictive power of the 11-plus IQ test is now said to result, not from its reflection of innate intelligence, but because social conditions have largely determined the child's educability by the age of 11. Much was heard in happier times about the correlation between IQ scores and teachers' opinions of pupils, but the report has now to admit that all sorts of extraneous personal factors may influence the teacher's assessment of his charges. Psychological theories which had given support to streaming in schools and to the provision of several types of secondary school are overturned completely, the report resisting both any attempt to stream pupils within schools before the age of 13, and any similar attempt to segregate pupils into different types of secondary school. Comprehensive schools, at least up to that age, are therefore seen as preferable to the existing system. By now, however, whether to collapse or to fight the wave against the tripartite system and the 11-plus selection was a question of no importance for the stout-hearted British psychologists. Comprehensive schooling was by now unstoppable, whatever they might say to the contrary, or even, amazingly, in its favour. When Simon pressed his attack there were ten comprehensive schools in the whole country: at the time this work is being written, they form the overwhelming bulk of British state schools.

The Under-critical Model

The history of the foregoing sections may now be analysed using the by now familiar concepts of error cost, sensitivity of policy to conjecture and critical level. Until about 1950 theories of educational psychology had a very low, often zero, error cost. Adopting IQ tests as a method of selecting children for free secondary school places leads to more or less the same choices being made as when the earlier methods of formal examination and teachers' reports were used. IQ testing therefore changes little in the world. If the conjectures of educational psychology which support IQ tests are accepted, the same children go to the same schools as when the conjectures are rejected. This is, as we have seen, a typical case where ideas from educational psychology were used to rationalize existing policies, giving them a zero error cost. The policy of selection for free secondary places is therefore completely insensitive to the conjectures of educational psychology; the truth or falsity of these theories makes no difference to the final selection which is made, and similarly for the other cases where it might seem that psychology was an influence on policy: the ending of primary education at 11, the types of secondary school provided, and streaming within schools.

Where error is expensive, it makes sense to search for it energetically; where mistakes are cheap a more relaxed level of criticism is appropriate. It is therefore not surprising to find that during the first period of our history of British educational psychology, 1900–50, its conjectures were submitted to a very low level of scrutiny. Here is the explanation for the ready acceptance of the papers of Cyril Burt, although the present-day reader can only be shocked at their sloppiness. Burt's exposure as a fake came very late in the history given here—1973. It is clear that his studies of separated identical twins reported in various papers in the 1950s and 1960s were fictitious, and that his results on the regression to the mean of IQ scores in 1961 are an invention. It is not clear just how early in his very long career Burt took to deception, but this is not really the point at issue. Burt's papers are often extremely poorly written, with, for example, no indication of methodology or sometimes even of the test administered to his subjects; and with the most inadequate referencing to earlier work where, it is claimed, these details may be found. Even if these earlier articles are all genuine, they could only have become a central part of educational psychology if read with the most friendly eye. This is, of course, just what happened. Criticism of Burt's work, like criticism of educational psychology generally, suited no-one at the time, and so it received no real scrutiny. The passage from research paper to sanctification in text books was quite painless.

The case of British educational psychology from 1900 to 1950 is an example of what was called in Chapter 4 the under-critical model of the relationship between science and policy. A consensus on policy makes for widespread agreement about conjectures which support the policy. These conjectures therefore receive very little criticism, appearing far more sound than they would otherwise. The apparent soundness of the conjectures feeds back into policy, for the existing policy seems so well suited to the facts revealed by science that it is hard to change it. Existing policies are therefore reinforced, for dissent now involves tackling science as well. Thus, a policy consensus generates a technical consensus. If there is still the shadow of a doubt that the ready acceptance of educational psychology in this period comes from the scientific soundness of psychological research and not from its conformity with the policy consensus of the day, just remember how rapidly psychological theories were revised when the agreement over policy collapsed after 1950.

Analysis of the IQ debate in America in the previous chapter shows that it fits the over-critical model, like the debate on the effects of lead on health. The error cost of psychological conjectures such as those proposed by Jensen are high and intense criticism is therefore applied to them. Moreover, criticism is particularly easy because of the loss of autonomy central to the hopes of educational psychology to provide useful guidance to teachers and policymakers, and because of interdisciplinary problems of communication and research. Debate on technical issues therefore becomes endless; if any issues are closed through research findings, it is only at the cost of raising half a dozen new questions. Disagreement over policy generates technical debate in these cases. The lack of technical consensus means that the results of research cannot influence policy; any findings that threaten to influence policy are immediately entangled in a whole network of criticism.

Where technical debate stands in the way of theories such as Jensen's influencing American education policy, the lack of technical debate in Britain before 1950 similarly bars any influence of British research on British education policy. Technical consensus only existed because of the low error cost of the conjectures put forward by educational psychologists at this time, which meant that policy was completely insensitive to the conjectures. This is the dilemma facing scientific research which hoped to be relevant to policy. If it is relevant, if policy is sensitive to some conjecture, then the conjecture has a high error cost and will generate an endless technical argument preventing it from affecting policy. On the other hand, if the conjecture supports an existing policy consensus, it will have a low error cost and will escape criticism, but only at the cost of having no influence on policy.

In the under-critical model, conjectures of science appear to be very successful; there is, after all, a consensus among the experts, but success is an illusion which evaporates whenever the consensus over policy which suppresses criticism breaks down. The function of the scientific results is to support the agreement over policy and to make it harder for dissent to arise. In the present case, why such a noise about educational psychology when it had so little real influence on the conduct of education? The psychologists' theories and tests were weapons in the battle of interests between the middle and the working class and between parents and teachers, serving to entrench the existing consensus. Should the Labour Party or parents' groups wish to undo the existing consensus, then they would have to take on not just their political foes, but science itself. There is therefore no surprise in the events after 1950 when changing times and shifts in the balance of power swept away the long-established agreements about the way British children should be educated. With free places for all children at secondary schools, the political issues of the day becomes one of the manner in which children are picked out as suitable for one type of school or another. The error cost of educational psychology's theories of testing had suddenly taken a large leap. If the psychologists were correct, then children would be distributed to schools partly on the basis of their IQ scores in the 11-plus examination, but if the conjectures of the scientists were false, the whole rationale of separate types of school would disappear and comprehensive schools would be the best solution. Educational policy therefore becomes very sensitive to psychological theory; the basic question of the tripartite system with 11-plus selection versus comprehensive schools depended on it. As had happened from a much earlier date in the United States, this rise in error cost led to the views of the psychologists being subjected to intense critical scrutiny, in complete contrast to the happy consensus of earlier decades. The debate about education policy produced a corresponding argument about the results of psychology which were thought relevant to policy; and the under-critical model was transformed into the over-critical one, as British interest in the technical debates in America increased.

10 Smoking and Lung Cancer

The final case study is an example like the last one which, at a superficial level, threatens to falsify the sceptical thesis of this book by providing an instance where policy has been strongly influenced by the results of scientific research; it concerns the connection between scientific evidence about the causes of lung cancer and policy against smoking. As before, it is hoped that scepticism will triumph upon a closer examination of the story.

The Technical Debate

The smoking and health debate involved a range of diseases and health effects, but for reasons of space this study is confined to the debate about smoking as a cause of lung cancer. The study is further confined to the debate in Britain, although similar conflicts occurred in America and many other countries. A full discussion is given in Reeve (1985), and so the present treatment can be brief. The scientific debate can conveniently be seen as starting in the early 1950s with the publication of the first results from a retrospective study of the smoking habits of lung cancer victims by Doll and Hill (1950). The Medical Research Council (1957), noting an increase in lung cancer, looked for the causes of this increase. They argued that the evidence pointed to a close association between smoking and lung cancer and that the most reasonable interpretation of this relationship was that it was causal. The evidence consisted of the retrospective studies mentioned above—comparing past histories of lung cancer sufferers and non-sufferers—prospective studies looking at the smoking habits of defined groups in the population and studying the causes of death occurring subsequently in the group, and laboratory experiments which had identified carcinogens in tobacco smoke. The Research Council's statement was endorsed by the *British Medical Journal* (1957), the official organ of the British Medical Association, which went on to propose measures to reduce the smoking habit. Since then there have been three reports from the Royal College of Physicians (1962, 1971, 1977), which represent milestones in the medical profession's case against smoking.

A rival hypothesis accounting for the accepted association between smoking and lung cancer was proposed by, among others, the eminent statistician, geneticist and biometrician, Sir Ronald Fisher (1958). The suggestion was that the same genes may predispose an individual to both lung cancer and smoking. As the debate between those supporting a causal theory and those supporting a genetic one developed, emphasis was placed by each side on evidence which appeared decisive in supporting one theory and conflicting with the other. In this way a number of crucial issues emerged on which the debate centred. Most important among these were the following:

1. The critics of the causal theory placed emphasis on the early epidemiological studies which had shown that smokers who inhaled had a lower risk of lung cancer than those who did not.
2. The critics of the genetic theory emphasized the observation that when male British doctors reduced their cigarette consumption, their lung cancer mortality rate fell relative to the rest of the male population and in correspondence with their reduced cigarette consumption.
3. The critics of the causal theory emphasized the need for studies of identical and non-identical twins to test the genetic component in smoking and in lung cancer and some support for the genetic theory came from these studies.
4. The critics of the genetic theory emphasized the observation of a large recorded increase in deaths from lung cancer which could hardly reflect a change in the population's genes.

The whole debate, cannot be covered here; space restricts any detailed discussion of its development to two of these crucial issues—the inhalation problem and the effect of giving up smoking.

(a) *The Inhalation Problem*

Doll and Hill (1950) showed a negative correlation between inhaling and lung cancer. Fisher (1958) concentrated on this point as it can be dealt with by the genetic hypothesis but it seems to conflict with the causal hypothesis. Fisher concluded that Doll and Hill's data on inhaling falsified the theory that smoking is a cause of lung cancer, leading him to question the conclusions which the Medical Research Council had come to in their statement on smoking and lung cancer. Fisher argued that they were jumping from the observation of an association to the conclusion of a causal relationship. To emphasize this point he argued that if the Medical Research Council made this jump in the case of cigarette smoking they should also make it in the case of inhaling, and this would lead to the conclusion that cigarette smoking causes lung cancer but inhaling cigarette smoke prevents it.

This problem for the causal theory became a key issue in the debate, being repeatedly referred to by the opponents of the causal theory. Eysenck *et al.* (1960) presented some evidence in support of the genetic hypothesis. In criticizing the causal hypothesis the authors refer to the problem that inhaling appears to have an ameliorating effect with respect to lung cancer. In an exchange following this paper, between Eysenck and 'Geminus' (1960a) of *New Scientist*, Eysenck (1960) again referred to the inhalation problem. To this 'Geminus' (1960b) replied that at least three studies, other than the early Doll and Hill one, had shown a greater risk of lung cancer among inhalers. In their first report, the Royal College of Physicians (1962) admitted that there was some conflicting evidence on the effects of inhalation of smoke, but by the time of the publication of the second report, 1971, the Royal College concluded that inhaling increased the risk of lung cancer. The issue arose again, however, with the description of his views on the smoking and lung cancer debate by Burch (1974). Here he refers to Fisher's findings on inhaling, claiming that they still represent a serious problem for the causal theory. In a reply to this paper, Doll (1974) suggested that the figure on inhalation used by Burch was atypical. He further argued that an explanation for the apparent anomaly had been provided nearly twenty years previously by C. N. Davies. This explanation was that deep inhalation does not deposit smoke droplets on the walls of the bronchii, which is where lung cancer usually occurs. Doll concludes that until enough is known about the physical distribution of tobacco droplets in the respiratory tract of different types of smokers, the data on inhaling remains open to debate.

Doll and Peto (1976) gives the final results of the twenty-year investigation of the smoking habits of male British doctors. Concerning the inhaling issue, they again admit that some conflicting evidence exists, but they point out that some studies suffer from lack of standardization for amount smoked and that the distinction between inhaling and not-inhaling is not absolute. They conclude that it is impossible to interpret the results on inhaling until more information is available on the fate of smoke droplets.

The inhaling issue is discussed in Royal College of Physicians (1977), their third report. Acknowledging that several studies have shown that among heavy smokers inhalers have a slightly lower risk of lung cancer than non-inhalers, the report suggests two explanations for this. Either statements about inhaling are inaccurate or deep inhalation deposits smoke in parts of the lung that are less susceptible to cancer. The issue crops up again, however, in Eysenck (1980) where the inhalation problem is used to criticize the causal theory. In criticizing this book Peto (1980) argues that Eysenck uses outdated evidence on the inhalation issue, ignoring more recent evidence which provides an explanation for the apparent anomaly. Evidence published in 1978 purported to show that heavy smokers who say they do not inhale are actually 'slow' inhalers, and those who say they do inhale are 'fast' inhalers. Fast inhalation may cause less tar to be deposited in the upper airways which are most susceptible to cancer.

The history of this issue shows how it was first highlighted by the opponents of the causal theory who saw it as a serious problem for that theory. But as these critics repeatedly emphasized this issue the causal theorists developed various explanations for the apparent anomaly and placed emphasis on the inconclusive nature of the evidence. These explanations finally led to new types of research into the accuracy of statements about inhaling, although the question is still far from closed.

(b) *The Effect of Giving Up Smoking*

Doll and Hill (1964) present results of their long-running study of the smoking habits and deaths from lung cancer among British doctors. They interpreted the results as showing, among other things, that in men who had given up cigarette smoking the death rate from lung cancer had fallen. The authors maintain that this can only be explained in terms of the causal and not the genetic hypothesis. Royal College of Physicians (1971), their second report, placed emphasis on this evidence as a serious problem for the genetic hypothesis. The report argues that on the genetic hypothesis the inborn liability and hence incidence of lung cancer should be unaffected by persuading people to resist their desires and stop smoking. Following the report, an editorial in *The Lancet* (1971) placed emphasis on the evidence that stopping smoking reduced the risk of lung cancer, seeing it as an important weapon against the genetic hypothesis.

The presentation of this evidence in the second Royal College report was subject to a close examination and critical assessment in Seltzer (1972a) which argues that certain difficulties with the interpretation of secular trends were ignored by the Royal College report, and that diseases had been grouped into the categories 'related' and 'unrelated' to smoking in a different way from the Doll and Hill study on which their analysis heavily relied, without any explanation for the change. More seriously, Seltzer pointed out that the report had used data for only two of the three time periods in the original study and for only one of the two age groups. He also argued that the data did not support the report's claim that there was little change in the smoking habits of the general population comparable to the change observed among doctors. After a re-examination of the data, including both age groups and all three time periods, plus further data on the smoking habits of the general population, Seltzer concluded that the statements and claims of the Royal College Report, based on the particular set of data which they cited, could not be supported.

In an editorial accompanying this article *The Lancet* (1971) suggested that several of Seltzer's criticisms were unimportant and the more serious ones it called into question. It attempted to provide some justification for the Royal College Report's omissions of data and accused Seltzer of missing out the most crucial time period. Seltzer is accused of confusing the issue, but has failed to throw any doubt on the main conclusion that the data on British doctors provides strong evidence that stopping smoking increases the expectation of life. The article by Seltzer sparked off a series of correspondence in the columns of *The Lancet*, including letters from Doll (1972) and Fletcher (1972) arguing that *The Lancet* editorial had successfully shown the weakness of Seltzer's arguments. Seltzer (1972b) provides a detailed reply to the editorial, reiterating his criticism that the Royal College of Physicians' Report's claim rests on an inaccurate statement, namely that during the cited time periods, cigarette smoking declined among British doctors, but not in the population as a whole. The issue arises again in Burch (1974) which criticizes Doll and Hill's findings along the same lines as Seltzer. Burch found that over a particular time period the upper age group actually showed a considerable increase in lung cancer mortality and he suggests, with tongue in cheek, that retired doctors should have been warned of the dangers of giving up smoking. He attributes the various fluctuations in the trends involved for different age groups to diagnostic errors producing spurious trends.

In reply, Doll (1974) maintains that Burch has quoted only a subset of the figures which gives a different picture from the whole, arguing that, although there are some irregularities in the figures, the contrast between doctors and all men is marked and the evidence weighs against the genetic hypothesis. Burch replied by emphasizing the inconsistencies in the evidence for doctors, maintaining that the data showed that a large increase in recorded death rates accompanied an increase in the proportion of ex-smokers. He concluded that a comparison between the different populations of doctors and 'all men', as employed in the Doll and Hill comparison, was fraught with dangers. In a correspondence following these articles, Seltzer (1974) criticized Doll, using the same arguments he had presented earlier. He argued that Doll's use of facts and his comparison between British doctors and the general population were both faulty. The facts, according to Seltzer, contradict the causal hypothesis and this calls for 'dispassionate examination' rather than 'unsubstantiated rhetoric'.

Doll and Peto (1976) present the final results from the twenty-year study of British doctors. They make the observation that lung cancer grew relatively less common as the study progressed, while other cancers did not, corresponding to a reduction in cigarette consumption during the period of observation, and this, they claim, illustrates the causal nature of the association between smoking and lung cancer. An editorial (*British Medical Journal*, 1976), commenting on this paper, mentions this observation as a significant one. Burch (1978a) again argues that comparisons between temporal trends of mortality from lung cancer in doctors and the dissimilar population of England and Wales, with dissimilar standards of diagnosis, is inadmissible, and that Doll and Peto's own analysis only shows an average reduction in 'relative' mortality of doctors versus men, whereas the data suggests that the recorded and verified 'absolute' death rates from lung cancer in British male doctors have shown no significant temporal trend up or down over the period 1955–71. He argues that since the consumption of cigarettes by male doctors fell by more than 50 per cent in this period, it appears that doctors have derived little or no benefit with respect to lung cancer, or to all causes of death, by giving up cigarettes. Royal College of Physicians (1977), being their third report, reviewed the evidence related to the effects of stopping smoking, particularly that presented by Doll and Peto. The report gives as one of the main reasons for rejecting the genetic hypothesis that it fails to account for the relative decline in mortality from lung cancer among doctors.

In this discussion of a paper given by Burch (1978b) to the Royal Statistical Society, in which he presents further criticisms of the causal theory, Seltzer (1978) provides another criticism of the studies involving ex-smokers. These, he claims, are all flawed because the groups they involved were self-selected. Following this line of thinking, Eysenck (1980) presents the results of studies on the characteristics of smokers, non-smokers, successful and unsuccessful givers-up. It was found, Eysenck argues, that those who give up successfully are constitutionally more like non-smokers, while those who fail to give up smoking are constitutionally more like smokers. This, he claims, is an important finding since it shows that smokers and former smokers are not comparable groups. He concludes that genetic factors not only predispose people to smoke, but also determine the ease with which they can give up smoking. In criticizing Eysenck's book, Peto (1980) argues that he has misinterpreted the results of the Doll and Hill study concerning doctors' smoking habits, and his conclusion that the effects of giving up smoking did not support the view that giving up protects against lung cancer is in direct opposition to the facts.

The development of this issue illustrates some of the same points as the inhaling issue. A piece of evidence was interpreted by one side in such a way that it appeared to be decisive in supporting one theory—in this case the causal—against the genetic theory. Since this evidence was publicized as a decisive confirmation of the causal theory, its critics immediately called that interpretation into question. For the most part the data itself was accepted, but the use of that data and its interpretation were questioned. In fact in this case it was suggested that the interpretation could be turned completely on its head; where the Royal College of Physicians had argued that the data showed that giving up smoking reduced the risk of lung cancer, Burch argued that they appeared to show that giving up smoking increased the risk of lung cancer. The debate continued with a re-examination of the evidence and with further evidence being considered. Then, with the appearance of a possible explanation of the evidence in terms of the genetic theory, a new type of study was conducted whose results appear to support this explanation. The history of both issues considered here exemplifies this pattern: the identification of some evidence by one side with a decisive interpretation; the presentation of an alternative interpretation of the same evidence by the other side; a long debate on the merits and validity of each interpretation calling on extra evidence; the development of new types of research to test the various interpretations. This pattern is not unique to the two cases described above, but is common to all the crucial issues which emerged in the smoking and lung cancer debate but which time prevents us from considering in any great detail.

The pattern of these technical debates should not come as a surprise at this point in the discussion, for it mirrors the deadlock we have observed in the debates over the effects of lead on health and the inheritance of IQ. The debate about lung cancer and smoking seems as long-lived, for it began in the early 1950s, and is far from settled today. It involves scientific research which lost autonomy and disciplinarity by trying to settle a matter of urgent policy which requires work by scientists of all disciplines—epidemiologists, statisticians, biochemists, chemists, physiologists, and more besides. Relevance to policy gives conjectures about the health effects of smoking a much higher error cost than is customary for theories which remain in the realm of pure science, these conjectures therefore being subjected to much greater critical scrutiny than normal, as is obvious in the brief extracts from the technical debate considered here. No sooner is some new piece of evidence pronounced as conclusive support for one view than it is questioned by the other side, the debate expanding rather than contracting as time goes on.

Debate is not, after all, about technical fine points concerning the prevention of cancer, for the defenders of the genetic view are questioning the deepest model of disease enshrined in medical orthodoxy: that the body is healthy until some outside agent interferes with its functioning, be it a bacterium or a chemical from tobacco smoke, health being maintained by acting against the external agent. The genetic view would replace this by a model where many disorders are caused by the sufferer's genetic constitution, lung cancer being chosen as a topical instance of the more general claim. Such a theory would involve radical changes in medical treatment and, far deeper, changes in the very conception of disease and treatment, giving a place of prominence to the statistical detection of genetic features of the population, which perhaps explains the popularity of the genetic model among statisticians and psychologists who employ similar methods, as we have seen in the study on the inheritance of intelligence. A further feature of the present debate, revealed by even the brief discussion allowed to us, is the operation of selective citation, each side scanning the available evidence in order to make a case rather than assessing each item of evidence on its scientific merits. The next step, of course, is to consider the relevance of all this technical argument to policy about smoking.

Policy

The striking point about British policy concerning smoking is that very early, by about 1957, a consensus was established in all branches of government, mediated by their technical advisers, that smoking causes lung cancer. No major challenge to this consensus has come from the tobacco industry, although we have seen that the technical debate between the causal and genetic theories has continued from these early days to the present. For some reason the tobacco industry and its allies were unable to mobilize the attack on the causal hypothesis mounted by Fisher, Eysenck, Burch, Seltzer and others, for which we may be thankful since it offers a way of testing the scepticism about science and policy which is the central thesis of this book. Upholders of the conventional view that science may at times be highly relevant to policy will be strongly tempted to see the present case study as a prime example of the power of research to inform policy. On this view, the genetic hypothesis is an indefensible position overwhelmed by the objectively demonstrable superiority of the theory that lung cancer is caused by smoking: the consensus in government reflects the argument of its technical advisers about the merits of the causal theory. Those who continue to support the genetic view are cranks who defend the indefensible through their own personal commitment, no longer deserving of the title 'scientists'. In contrast, the sceptical view is that the technical debate about smoking and lung cancer is as intractable as the earlier ones about lead and intelligence. Given the shortcomings of research on smoking and the intensity of the critical scrutiny which its results receive, the debate between the causal and the genetic acounts is potentially endless. The consensus in government is to be explained on political, not scientific grounds. What prevents the tobacco industry from exploiting the case made out by defenders of the genetic hypo-thesis is not the scientific superiority of the rival causal theory, but the disposition of the political forces which bear on smoking policy. If these forces can be revealed—which is the purpose of the remaining pages of this chapter—then scepti-cism has triumphed over the traditional view which sees science as a natural handmaiden of policy.

Ian Macleod, the then Minister of Health, made the first government statement about smoking and lung cancer in 1954, being advised by the Standing Advisory Committee on Cancer and Radiotherapy, a body dominated by medical professionals. Macleod (1954) reported the association between cancer and smoking, but calmed people by pointing out the great uncertainties which existed over the inter-pretation of the data. Despite pressure from the Advisory Committee and many MPs, the Government took no imme-diate action towards a public information campaign. A similar tune was heard from the tobacco industry which pointed out that there was much work to be done before a causal relation-ship could be established, and emphasized the role of air pol-lution in causing lung cancer. To further this work, they donated £250,000 to the Medical Research Council. The tactics of the industry were to question the causal case made out by the medical profession, to call for more research and to stress their own responsible attitude in funding this work.

Those pushing for government action against smoking—the Standing Medical Advisory Committee, the Central Health Services Council, many MPs and the Chief Medical Officer of the Ministry of Health, Sir George Godber—were aided by the publication of Medical Research Council (1957), a report reviewing the epidemiological and laboratory evidence, con-cluding that the most reasonable interpretation is that smok-ing causes cancer, an opinion immediately endorsed in the editorial pages of the *British Medical Journal* (1957), the offi-cial organ of the British Medical Association. The report received immediate endorsement from the Government, Vaughan-Morgan (1957), a junior Health Minister, promising to bring this 'latest authoritative opinion' to the attention of the public through a programme of health education administered by local government. From then on, government policy has remained essentially fixed. Whatever minor changes have since been made have been built around the same central decision that the government's task is limited to that of telling people of the risks of smoking, enabling them to make an informed choice about their tobacco habits, and to protect young people who cannot make such a choice. In the words of Vaughan-Morgan (1957) 'Once the risks are known everyone who smokes will have to measure them and make up his or her own mind, and must be relied upon, as a responsible person, to act as seems best.'

There was naturally a discussion of a whole range of policies which could ameliorate the problem: the banning of smoking in public places, bans on advertising, searching for alternative means of tax revenue, but the government's position did not change from that of 1957, at least until 1962, action being delegated to local authorities to inform the public of the hazards of cigarette smoking. In a few places, local authorities went a little further, for example establishing withdrawal clinics and banning smoking in public places: a few clinics were set up by charitable societies, but the response was generally one of trying to educate the public as to the risks, passing on the decision of whether or not to smoke to the individual.

In the early period of policy formation, roughly 1953 to 1962, the tobacco industry, as we have seen, chose to fight the technical case made out by the proponents of the causal theory, forming the Tobacco Research Council (originally the Tobacco Manufacturer's Standing Committee) in 1956 to engage in research on lung cancer and smoking, and having its own laboratories by 1962. Sir Ronald Fisher, a past president of the Royal Statistical Society and an early supporter of the genetic hypothesis, was appointed as consultant to the Research Council. Earlier, Fisher had argued that the government had been prematurely persuaded of the causal hypothesis, whose shortcomings would be seen when a rival theory arrived.

The year 1962 saw the publication of what Friedman (1975) regards as the single most important document in the whole story, the first Report of the Royal College of Physicians, *Smoking and Health*, which reviewed all the evidence and concluded that smoking was a major cause of lung cancer, bronchitis and perhaps coronary heart disease. Recommendations made in the report include product modification to reduce noxious chemicals to tobacco smoke, public education, more effective restrictions on sales to minors, limiting tobacco advertising, higher taxes on cigarettes, the establishment of anti-smoking clinics, and so on. Massive publicity was given to the report: Enoch Powell (1962), then Minister of Health, accepted its 'authoritative and crushing demonstration' of the causal connection between smoking and cancer. The Chief Medical Officer of the Ministry of Health, Sir George Godber, stated in his annual report (Ministry of Health, 1963), 'This reviewed the evidence dispassionately and, with scrupulous fairness, stated conclusions which were wholly damning against cigarette smoking. There is surely no longer need to argue whether, but only how, the habit should be avoided or broken.'

In keeping with their offensive tactics during this period, the tobacco industry, through its Research Council, launched a vigorous attack on the technical case made out in the report, calling for much more research before intelligent policy could be made. From 1962 onwards, however, there is an important shift in the story. The government consensus that smoking causes lung cancer was maintained and deepened, but the technical opposition put up by the industry gradually faded to insignificance, its attack on the Royal College's first report being in effect its last extensive statement against the causal hypothesis.

Since about 1962 the industry has said that it does not make medical judgements, leaving these to qualified medical experts, although at times this policy has been contradicted by some of the Tobacco Research Council's statements. It seems that the industry is prepared to join the government and the medical profession in accepting the causal hypothesis, but only as a working assumption, emphasis being given to the need for further research and the commissioning of studies which highlight the role of factors other than smoking in the causation of lung cancer, such as air pollution. This is a much weaker line than the vigorous criticism made from the standpoint of the genetic hypothesis by Fisher and others. Dissent is heard, as we have seen, in academic publications, but the Tobacco Research Council has not picked up these voices for use in its defence of the tobacco industry. The technical case against the causal hypothesis has been placed very much 'on the back burner' in this part of the story, although it is clearly being kept in reserve should its revival ever be needed. While the Tobacco Research Council continues to emphasize the role of other agents in lung cancer, its criticisms of the medical profession's position have become much less vigorous and outspoken, and much of their own research has proceeded on the working hypothesis that smoking causes lung cancer— although this happy consenus may not last for ever. The Council's Chairman, for instance, has spoken of accepting the causal hypothesis to aid liaison with medical researchers. In 1976 the Tobacco Research Council declared agnosticism about the causal hypothesis. In the words of its Chairman, Sir Clifford Jarratt (1977), 'it is appropriate for the health authorities ... to look at the evidence and do the interpretation'. Tobacco was taken up as a case study in preventive medicine by the Parliamentary Expenditure Committee (1977), hearing representatives from all those concerned with smoking, including the industry. It reported that 'none of our witnesses doubted that cigarette smoking was the main cause of lung cancer'.

How is this shift in the tobacco industry's technical views to be interpreted? Is it that the causal hypothesis is so palpably superior to the genetic one that even the industry has to admit it, or is it that, the political forces being what they were, the industry no longer needed the genetic hypothesis to defend its interests? This is, of course, the key question of the whole chapter. The answer, to be developed below, is the latter. The continuing technical debate shows that it was possible for anyone who might wish to, to maintain a defence of the genetic hypothesis, without breach of scientific proprieties. The tobacco industry's refusal to adopt the defence can only be because its own position is so strong that it does not need to do so. This has now to be demonstrated.

The hidden factor now appears: the Treasury, together with other revenue departments, receives a very large and easily collectable tax on tobacco, which provides a very useful regulator, demand for tobacco being very inelastic. The

Treasury is obviously a very powerful political actor and has always been, behind the scenes, an ally of the tobacco industry. Right from the beginning, radical controls on smoking, such as banning of cigarettes, were simply not politically feasible because of the Treasury's influence, and were not seriously discussed. Government policy has always avoided rigorous controls by leaving the choice of whether to smoke to individuals, the government's task being merely to inform people of the hazards involved in smoking.

A good illustration of the predominance of economics over health in the formulation of government policy on smoking is provided by the one attempt to co-ordinate policy in this area—a committee of officials from the Department of Health and Social Security, the Scottish Home and Health Departments, the Treasury, the Department of Trade and Industry, Customs and Excise and the Central Statistical Office, meeting in 1971. Although their report was not published, it is known in some detail. There was no agreement on anti-smoking policy except to recommend a more extensive campaign of health education. The benefits of reducing lung cancer (and other) deaths by a 20 to 40 per cent drop in cigarette consumption are calculated in terms of lives saved, but against this in the balance is the extra pension paid to people living longer, an increase in demand for imports (worsening the balance of payments), a loss of tax revenue and increased unemployment in depressed areas of the country. To the extent that these calculations reflect thinking in the government generally, the government has accepted that cigarettes cause cancer, but economic considerations have prevented serious controls of the hazard.

Attempts by government to impose controls on smoking by negotiating voluntary agreements have also strengthened the political position of the tobacco industry, indeed Popham (1981) talks of this being the industry's 'trump card'. Since 1962 pressure has grown for more controls and the industry, through the Tobacco Advisory Committee, has negotiated a number of gentlemen's agreements with the Department of Health and Social Security. Advertisements on television before 9.00 p.m. were banned under a voluntary agreement in 1962, although banned altogether by statute in 1965, followed by negotiations on ways of informing the public of smoking hazards, the developments of tobacco substitutes and additives, more bans on advertising, promotion by coupons, and so on. Not only do the negotiations give the industry direct access to the government's thinking, and an official platform for arguing about them, but they also provide the opportunity for accepting weak voluntary controls in place of stronger, legal ones. The 1971 negotiations over the printing of a health warning on tobacco products is a good example, for according to Popham (1981) a voluntary agreement to print a mild warning on cigarette packets was accepted, the government of the day in turn killing off a Private Member's Bill which threatened much stronger warnings on all smoking products. The low impact of these warnings on cigarette sales, when they were eventually printed, is a reminder of the political impossibility of imposing severe controls on tobacco, given the interests of the Treasury. In Royal College of Physicians (1977) the ineffectiveness of such warnings is sourly commented on, and the whole exercise of voluntary controls attacked since 'it is inconceivable that the manufacturers would voluntarily agree to a warning that might affect their sales'.

An important argument used by the industry in its negotiations over controls on advertising is that advertisements do not encourage more people to smoke, they merely encourage those who already smoke to change their brand, perhaps to one with a lower tar and nicotine level. Against this, those who argue for stronger controls on smoking maintain that advertising should be limited because it does persuade some non-smokers into the habit. The Department of Health and Social Security which does not wish to offend the Treasury by imposing severe controls on advertising has often found the argument about brand swopping a useful escape route. Although only modest controls have been placed on the industry's advertisements, tobacco companies have found many ways round them, such as the sponsorship of sporting and cultural events, the naming of racing cars and the advertising of cigars bearing the same name as a cigarette which cannot be directly advertised.

A further source of the tobacco industry's political strength during this period has been the development of tobacco substitutes. After taking independent advice on the safety of the new products, Imperial Tobacco's 'New Smoking Material' and Courtauld's 'cytrel', eleven new brands of cigarettes containing a quarter tobacco substitute were marketed in 1977. They were an instant and total commercial failure, at no small cost to their promoters; but apart from this the possibility of using tobacco substitutes must have strengthened the hand of the tobacco industry in the years leading up to the marketing calamity, from about 1966. There was even less incentive for the Department of Health and Social Security to offend the Treasury by placing severe controls on cigarette smoking if the problem was soon to be ameliorated with the introduction of safer substitutes for tobacco. A final element which gives additional strength to the tobacco industry is the diversification, initially into tobacco-related trades but later into food, beer, wines and spirits, packaging and plastics, engineering pumps and retailing. Friedman (1975) suggests that at least some of this process was a direct reaction to the threat of more severe controls on cigarettes.

All in all, therefore, the tobacco industry has never been seriously threatened by government controls on its products, through its alliance with the Treasury, the voluntary and negotiated nature of the controls that have been imposed, the many ways around controls on advertising and health warnings, the development of tobacco substitutes and low tar and nicotine brands of conventional cigarettes, and product diversification, which add up to a position of very great strength. The industry has never needed to attack the hypothesis that smoking causes lung cancer in order to defend its own interests, which explains its failure to attack the case made out by the theory's supporters in government and the medical profession and its neglect of the genetic counter-argument after the early 1960s. It is not that the causal theory was so firmly based on solid evidence that it was beyond attack or so superior to the genetic hypothesis that only cranks could remain unconvinced, for the technical debate between the two theories has been continuous since the first evidence linking smoking and lung cancer came to light. The tobacco industry's failure to fight the causal hypothesis is therefore a reflection of the political forces operating in the determination of anti-smoking policies and not a surrender to a scientific hypothesis so firmly established as to be beyond effective criticism.

Analysis

Formally, the acceptance of the causal hypothesis by the tobacco industry as well as the medical profession and government has a low error cost for the industry. The difference to the world made by the acceptance of the causal hypothesis is a meagre one indeed: ineffective health warnings, a few easily overcome restrictions on advertising, anti-smoking literature and smoking bans in a few public places which do little to reduce sales, all of which impose only the most modest cost on the tobacco industry, which can therefore happily agree to accept the causal hypothesis, with a few reservations. Smoking policy has a very low sensitivity to the causal hypothesis—accepting the hypothesis alters policy, but only very modestly. It is therefore quite appropriate for the industry to adopt a low level of criticism towards the causal hypothesis, which is exactly what we have found. The acceptance of the causal hypothesis in policy circles does not sustain bold, daring, challenging policies which severely threaten the interests of some of the actors in the game of policymaking.

The story does not end here, however, for something needs to be said about the consensus in government about the correctness of the causal hypothesis from 1957 to the present. Defenders of the conventional view that scientific results can sometimes be of importance in policymaking would presumably see the present case as a good illustration of their thesis, for scientific research appears to have led to a technical consensus that smoking causes lung cancer, on which government policy has been based ever since. On this view, the development of consensus in government about the best interpretation of the findings linking smoking and lung cancer would be seen as a fair, balanced, unbiased rational assessment of the evidence available at the time, despite the continued defence of the genetic hypothesis by a few cranks and misfits. This sanguine view is now to be questioned. It will be shown that the victory of the causal over the genetic hypothesis in government circles was not the result of a fair fight between them, rather that the process of policymaking was heavily rigged in favour of the causal view. Our suspicions ought to be aroused by the very short time taken for the consensus in government to emerge—only four to five years. Was this period really sufficient to demonstrate the superiority of the causal hypothesis so dramatically that no rival could be seriously considered, especially when the longevity of technical debates on IQ and lead are recalled?

Advice to government on the technical issues surrounding smoking and lung cancer was dominated by the medical profession. Key figures—various Ministers of Health, and later Secretaries of the Department of Health and Social Security—were advised by bodies such as the Standing Medical Advisory Committee, the Central Health Services Council, the Standing Advisory Committee on Cancer and Radiotherapy, which were dominated by medical people, not forgetting the important role played by Sir George Godber, the medically qualified Chief Medical Officer to the Ministry of Health. Contact between the Department of Health and Social Security and the medical profession is close and occurs at every level, so it is hardly surprising to find the Department using these channels to learn about the connection between smoking and cancer. Later, this was formalized with the establishment in 1971 of Action on Smoking and Health (ASH), funded largely by the Department as a pressure group and advisory and co-ordinating body and again dominated by medical professionals, some of whom were responsible for the very influential Royal College of Physicians' second and third Reports.

The close relationship between government and the medical profession unwittingly served as a filter against views unpalatable to the profession, in particular the genetic hypothesis. There were at least four factors involved here. Having discovered the statistical link between smoking and cancer, the medical profession had a vested interest in the connection being causal, for then action against smoking would reduce deaths from cancer and the profession would receive kudos and status in exchange for this benefit to society. Should the connection be genetic, it is hard to see what action might be taken to reduce the incidence of lung cancer.

Secondly, the causal model fitted the medical profession's model of disease: bodies are healthy unless acted upon by external agents such as viruses, bacteria or the chemicals in cigarette smoke. In addition, the medical profession has a well-known bias towards action rather than inaction, summed up in the motto 'if in doubt—treat', for there is generally less risk in the erroneous treatment of a healthy person than in neglecting to treat a sick one. Action against smoking was therefore likely to have been favoured by medical workers, even though the evidence for the causal hypothesis could still be questioned. The last point predisposing the profession to accept the causal theory is that its rival, the genetic theory, was proposed as a deliberate challenge not just to the one case of smoking and lung cancer, but to the whole medical model of disease. In its place, the defenders of the genetic view wanted to see a model which gave a far greater role to genes in the origin of disease. The view of the evidence on smoking taken by the medical profession must have been influenced by the threat implied in the genetic hypothesis.

Scientists are human: there are of necessity all sorts of pre-dilections, hopes and interests at play in the way evidence is interpreted. There is nothing extraordinary in the above case: the medical profession cannot be blamed for wanting to see the connection between cigarettes and health in a particular way. We generally hope, however, to find several groups of scientists taking different views of the evidence and arguing it out as best they may. The mythical unbiased scientist does not exist: the least we can do therefore is to pit the predilections of one against the biases of another. It was just this that was absent in the present case. Psychologists and statisticians were the main supporters of the view that smoking and the development of lung cancer are linked genetically, and this is no accident, for such a view gives great importance to the statistical analysis with which both are familiar. But the biases of this group were not pitched against the biases of the medical profession, for the tobacco industry did not care to defend the genetic hypothesis. The causal hypothesis of the medical advisers of government therefore received no challenge. Whenever this happens, the unchallenged hypothesis always looks far more powerful an explanatory instrument than it really is. One recalls here the theory of IQ defended by British educational psychologists which appeared hugely successful until challenged as the policy process rolled on. Research on the genetic hypothesis has, of course, continued in an academic environment, but how does this look from the point of view of government policymakers? Whatever the merits claimed for the hypothesis, the failure of the tobacco industry to defend it and fund its development must surely indicate how very weak it is. Its proponents are therefore seen as cranks—an inevitably consequence of scientific argument without power. There is therefore a serious bias in the policy process concerning smoking. It is not that the superiority of the causal theory silenced opposition, except for a few pseudo-scientists—the story that is traditionally told. Consensus was reached not by the defeat of rival opinions in free and open critical combat, but by the suppression of the genetic hypothesis by means of the filter provided by the medical profession—a bias which the powerful tobacco industry did not need to correct.

What effect did this bias in the assessment of rival explanations of the link between smoking and cancer have on policy? Recalling the discussion in Chapter 4: a good policy demands a realistic appraisal of the uncertainties which surround the factual issues relevant to policy, but in the present case this was absent. The uncertainties surrounding the causal hypothesis were understated while those surrounding its rival were exaggerated. The case which could be made out for the causal hypothesis was far weaker than it appeared to the government and its medical advisers to be. Had the genetic hypothesis been examined with the seriousness it deserved, with appropriate attention given to the results of well-funded research, much might have been learned about the genetic influence on disease in general and lung cancer in particular. Research in this direction might have been very fruitful, offering as it does a striking contrast to the orthodox models of medicine. Our understanding and treatment of disease might have been deepened by such an exercise, much more attention being paid, for example, to the search for genetic markers of diseases, and to the amelioration of symptoms of diseases of genetic origin. In suppressing the genetic case for lung cancer and cigarette smoking, the medical advisers to government and the medical profession in general ruled out what might have been a very fruitful line of inquiry, given the real uncertainties of the case.

What appears to be a political success for the medical profession may in this way have been bought at great cost. The profession's aims of understanding and treating illness and promoting good health might have been best served by much more thorough attention to the genetic model of illness in general and to the genetic link between smoking and lung cancer in particular. Their understanding of lung cancer and other diseases and their treatment might have been improved by this research, with consequent benefits to the profession, an avenue cut off by their political victory over the defenders of the genetic hypothesis.

11 Conclusions

The Over-critical Model

The principal conclusion of this work, from which the other points to be made in this chapter largely follow, is that the over-critical model of science applied to policymaking is a good account of reality. On this model, whenever science attempts to influence policy, three necessary conditions for efficient scientific research and analysis—autonomy, disciplinarity and a low level of criticism—are immediately broken, leading to endless technical debate rather than the hoped-for consensus which can limit arguments about policy. The technical debate concerns the interpetation to be given to the existing body of evidence, but no matter how large this body may be, widely divergent interpretations may be maintained, making argument practically endless. As debate continues, many long-settled technical issues are reopened for investigation, and attempts to definitely resolve one issue often succeed only in opening up many more technical issues for consideration; technical uncertainties grow rather than diminish as more research is done. Relevance to policy increases the level of criticism to which technical conjectures are submitted, and such criticism is even easier than usual since the loss of autonomy and the weakening of disciplinary boundaries produces research results of poor quality.

The over-critical model (described in Chapter 4) has been clearly instantiated in two of the case studies presented—lead (in Chapter 5) and IQ in the United States (in Chapter 8). A further supporting case has been given where, on a superficial level, a technical consensus existed about conjectures which appear relevant to policymaking, threatening falsification of the over-critical model. Closer analysis, however, revealed that the conjectures' influence on policy is really very slight, or even non-existent. The case is, of course, that of British educational psychology before the Second World War (Chapter 9). A second case which might falsify the over-critical model is smoking and lung cancer (in Chapter 10), where it seems that policy against smoking in Britain is built around the acceptance of the technical conjecture of a causal link between cigarette smoking and lung cancer. But there is an ongoing technical argument about the connection between smoking and lung cancer which shows all the signs of debates in cases which fit the over-critical model, the difference being that technical debate has in the present case become detached from the policy process. It suits all policy actors to agree that smoking causes lung cancer, despite the technical arguments, leaving the opponents of this conjecture to be labelled as cranks. As in the case of educational psychology in Britain, the cost of such ready acceptance of a conjecture is the conjecture's inability to influence policy. Policy is only marginally altered by the acceptance of the conjecture that smoking causes lung cancer, and so the over-critical model has resisted the falsification which a superficial examination of the case study threatened. To put things a little more formally: the over-critical model entails that there are no cases of technical consensus built up for a conjecture by free and open debate and inquiry, where the conjecture has a significant influence upon policy. Such conjectures have been searched for in all the case studies which have been presented, and yet none has been found. It must therefore be concluded that there is at least this much support for the over-critical model.

It should be noted that the over-critical model is at one and the same time descriptive of the influence of science on policy in the real world and prescriptive, giving guidance about how policy ought to be made—a double theme which runs through the whole work. In particular, the level of criticism which a conjecture receives not only varies with the use to which the conjecture is to be put, increasing with error cost, but the level of criticism ought to vary in just this way. It is rational to search vigorously for error when error is likely to be expensive; when mistakes are cheap, it is a waste of effort to be so scrupulous. The principle of relevance, holding that the degree of criticism received by a conjecture should reflect its use, therefore describes what goes on in the real world of policymaking, but also prescribes that, regardless of the real world, criticism should be adjusted to error cost. Cases where, for some reason, there is no attempt to criticize conjectures to which policy is sensitive will, on this prescription, produce poor decisions, poor by the very standards and interests of those making them.

The over-critical model tells us much about the intellectual status of science, which is exposed as a very tender plant, able to flourish under conditions of autonomy, disciplinarity and a low level of critical scrutiny. Only then can there be a consensus about solutions to the puzzles of normal science. The organization of science ensures that when these conditions are met, progress can be astonishingly fast, with problems being solved at a truly impressive rate. But the price for this power must be paid. When the conditions are not met, when research is directed from outside on problems where disciplinary distinctions are blurred, and where any proposed solution will have a high error cost, consensus is quite impossible. The price of a super-efficient normal science is the impossiblity of scientific research exerting any significant influence on policy decisions.

Incrementalism

It follows from the scepticism of the over-critical model that the myth of rationality is altogether unachievable, as was shown in the case of policy for the control of lead in the environment (in Chapter 6). Policy made in the way demanded by synoptic rationality makes enormous demands on scientific knowledge which, even without the problem posed by the over-critical model, are very expensive in terms of resources and time. The over-critical model is the final nail in the coffin of rationality, showing that, even with unlimited time and money, scientific research cannot be used to influence policy beyond the margin. Science cannot meet the demands made of it by upholders of the myth of rationality, nor by those who favour less extreme forms of the myth, such as mixed scanning.

None of these problems is faced by the incrementalist view of policymaking, championed by Lindblom, which sees decisions as the outcome of mutual adjustment between a group of partisans, each employing disjointed incrementalism to make his own decisions. Indeed, the chief advantage of the whole approach is that policy made in this way makes only the most modest demands upon scientific research and analysis, a point developed in the discussion of policy for the control of lead (in Chapter 7). Scepticism about the power of science to assist policymaking therefore strongly favours incrementalism. As before, it is important to remember that incrementalism is put forward at the same time as a description of actual practice in policymaking, and a prescriptive account of how policy ought to be made. The ways we have of making decisions seem to be successful, and their success can be explained by showing that the machinery of policymaking runs in something like the way that the ideal machine of incrementalism operates (in Chapter 4).

The merits of incrementalism may be restated in the light of this discussion. The distribution of power among a group of political actors with widely differing interests serves to limit the cost of errors in policy decisions. Whereas a single powerful actor might attempt over-radical, even revolutionary changes which impose huge costs if they do not perform as planned, the need to form a coalition in support of any policy limits decisions to marginal changes which, even if they are wrong, are not expensively so. Such damage limitation is the customary logic behind incrementalist accounts of the policy process. The logic may now be rephrased. Policymakers tend to favour technical conjectures which support their favoured policy and therefore misperceive such conjectures in a systematic way, understating the intensity of the criticism with which the conjectures should be examined and overstating their performance in resisting criticism. A single policymaker is therefore condemned to adopt policies which are sensitive to such conjectures. Insensitivity is the desired property of decisions, however, because of the inescapable fallibility of all technical conjectures. Poor decisions are therefore likely to come from a lone policymaker, poor by the actor's own standards, because a distorted view of the policy's error costs will be taken. If money is required, or happiness, then more money or more happiness are likely to result from adopting policies which are insensitive to technical conjectures rather than policies which are sensitive to them. Having many actors, each convinced of a set of conjectures which it finds to its own taste, overcomes the problem. Each actor wishes to convince the others of the truth of his own favoured conjectures, but failure is inevitable, provided that power is shared out more or less evenly. Policy must then be made by compromises between the actors, any compromise being highly insensitive to all technical conjectures. The machinery of policymaking thus ensures that the distorted perceptions of all the actors are automatically discounted and that the error cost of policy is less than it would have been had decisions been left to just one actor.

The Ironical Role of Science in Policymaking

To say that policies ought to be, and are, insensitive to scientific conjectures is not to say that there ought to be and that there is no role for science at all in decision-making. The case study on lead (in Chapter 7) shows how important it is to develop policy against a background of research through which any conjecture which might be relevant to policy may be criticized. Should one actor dominate the policy scene, then his own favourite interpretation of the available data will go largely unchallenged. Whatever criticism may be made by less powerful groups will easily be described as the work of cranks anxious to bend scientific results to their own political purposes. In this way, the interpretation of the dominant actor will look far more secure than it really is, so much so that it may be employed in policymaking without any serious reservations. Policy will then be highly sensitive to this particular interpretation of the evidence, whereas good policy—good according to the standards and interests of the actors in the policy drama—is insensitive to all scientific conjectures. Until the early 1960s, decisions on the control of lead in the working and general environment were dominated by the lead industry and their occupational hygienists, like Kehoe in America, who were happy to accept the threshold hypothesis that damage to health from lead occurs only when exposure takes the concentration of the metal in blood above 80 μg/100ml. This greatly eased their work in operating a hygienic plant and also allayed any alarm there might have been from the general public whose blood lead levels would never exceed this threshold without some quite extraordinary event—such as eating paint flakes or burning off leaded paint in a closed room day after day. Policy therefore came to be centred on the existence of this threshold figure.

The threshold conjecture looked completely solid until it was undermined by researchers in other fields who became increasingly worried about the subtle effects of much lower levels of the metal on health, those to which the normal population was frequently exposed. With hindsight, and after such argument, it now appears that the population considered by Kehoe and his fellow hygienist was so dissimilar to the general population, containing no children, no women, no old men, no male adolescents, no sick males, and so on, that nothing that might be said about the one can simply be said about the other. Even if the threshold hypothesis were correct for the working population, this says nothing about how lead might affect the wider population. Policy, and especially the disregard of any risk to the general public, was eventually seen to have been too sensitive to the threshold conjecture. A remedy would have been for other actors to conduct scientific research on the effects of lead on health on the general population much earlier, avoiding the dominance of the industrial hygienists. The argument between the hygienists and other researchers would then have been earlier and policy, being a compromise between supporters of both views, would have done something of a suitably marginal nature towards ameliorating any effect of lead on the general population much earlier than actually happened. Policy would then have been less sensitive to the conjecture about thresholds.

A further example is the case study on smoking (Chapter 10), where the political scene is dominated by medical professionals who favour the conjecture that smoking causes lung cancer. Other scientists deny this, arguing for some sort of genetic connection between the two, but their case is not now supported by the tobacco industry, whose interests are best served by more or less admitting a causal connection. Having no policy friends to protect them and advertise their case, the dissenters are easily discounted as cranks. It was argued that this produced poor policy because nobody wished to take up the genetic hypothesis, which not only might be true in the present case, but also offers a general line of attack against the medical model of disease. If the dissenters had more political support, their technical case would have to be taken more seriously and policy would have to be made by way of a compromise between upholders of the causal and the genetic hypotheses.

The role of scientific research and analysis is therefore not the heroic one of providing truths by which policy may be guided, but the ironic one of preventing policy being formulated around some rival technical conclusions. Research on one hypothesis ought to cancel out research on others, enabling policy to be made which is insensitive to all scientific conjectures. The work of the researchers who become concerned with lead poisoning in the general public eventually prevented Kehoe's threshold conjecture from guiding policy, and in turn Kehoe's conjecture prevented too much weight being given to the new research findings in the formulation of policy. That is, of course, a very far cry from the noble task traditionally allotted to science in the making of the policy, where the twin myths of rationality and the power of science intertwine so intimately.

A final point for comment is that in the cases of lead and smoking where this balance has not been made, or was made only recently, we may speak of a bias in the policy process which matches the distortion of scientific research in favour of one conjecture against others. Bias in this sense is an objective, publically identifiable and publically remediable feature of the policymaking machine, not, according to traditional views, a subjective property of individual minds (Chapter 2).

The Under-critical Model

An important source of bias in policymaking has been described as the under-critical model where scientific experts defend and entrench existing agreements on policy by providing technical evidence which matches the political consensus. The clearest case is that of British educational psychology before 1950 (Chapter 9), whose theories of inherited IQ served the consensus on policy that education resources should be distributed in such a way as to favour middle-class children over those of the working class. On issues of political conflict, theories of psychology maintained a respectful silence: wherever consequences relevant to policy were drawn, they always managed to agree with the existing consensus on policy in the teaching profession, educational administration, and so on. When IQ tests were sold as aids to selection for various types of school at 11-plus, the key point was that the tests made the same selection of pupils as did existing means of allocating school places. There was no attempt to improve selection, for the news that teachers had been doing it wrong for years was a threat to their acceptance of educational psychology. But the example may not be typical in all respects. In particular, when the consensus on policy changed in the early 1950s, with the idea of comprehensive education without the need for an 11-plus selection procedure gathering more and more supporters, the collapse of the British educational psychologists was sudden and complete, as they tried to identify a new role for themselves in the comprehensive system. From this, it might be inferred that the ideas of the psychologists were merely an adornment to policy, and that they had no real influence in delaying the policy change from selection to comprehensive education when its time had come. Whatever opinion may be held on this point, it would be dangerous to generalize them to other cases. The change in consensus about the British educational system was swift and powerful, not resistible at all by the educational psychologists; but in less extreme cases, experts whose conjectures serve a particular consensus on policy can in fact extend its life by absorbing minor episodes of doubt and criticism.

In the light of the discussion in the previous section, it is clear that the under-critical model is detrimental to policymaking. The whole function of the scientific theories thrown up by the experts in such cases is to suppress criticism of an existing political agreement, for any attack must now be aimed at scientists as well as political actors. But good policymaking requires openness to criticism, in particular the ability to question the technical evidence cited in support of a policy option. Without this, policy may well unwittingly be highly sensitive to some technical conjectures whose real uncertainties are disguised and therefore greatly understated. A technical consensus which supports an earlier political agreement does exactly this—its conjectures seem very powerful, but only because criticism from rival technical perspectives is suppressed. Anyone who is so bold to ask such questions threatens not only the theory but the political consensus which employs it. Alternatives to policy are not therefore explored, and in particular scientific research which might show the road to such alternatives is suppressed.

The Extraordinary Case of the Dutch Bells

A news article in the *Scientific American* of September 1985 reports a troubling story from the Netherlands where ancient bells have been slowly changing their pitch over the last few years. Since many of the country's bells are hung in carillons, the problem is not confined to the experts of the bell-ringing world. Acid rain has been suggested as the culprit. Sulphur dioxide, created by burning fossil fuels, is thought to dissolve in the rainwater which fall on the bells, slowly dissolving their surface, and altering their pitch. We are told that more research on this strange pollution phenomenon is being undertaken by the Dutch authorities. For all its parochial aspects, the story contains many lessons about how policy problems with technical aspects should be conceived. The problem of the bells is presented as one whose solution requires first, the identification of the cause and second, the amelioration of the origins of the problem through some suitable instrument of policy. Should acid rain prove to be the cause of the loss of tuning, then something must be done to reduce the quantity and corrosiveness of the polluted rain which falls from the Dutch sky. This conception of the problem makes great demands on scientific research, indeed, ones which are quite impossible. Discounting the problems which arise from the over-critical model, even if a scientific consensus on the acid rain conjecture could be achieved, it would consume a great deal of valuable resources, and take many years—during which time, what is to be done about the bells? Add to this the over-critical model, and the demands made of science are totally unrealistic. All the bells in the Netherlands would be dissolved and washed away to the North Sea long before any agreement could be reached about the causes of the phenomenon. The conception of the problem is also politically naive, for even if the cause could be identified as sulphur dioxide emissions, these emissions might originate from places far beyond the jurisdiction of the Netherlands Government, or if they are local, the emissions may be far too expensive to control, or control may be practically unfeasible. Learning this after years of expensive research into the causes of the carillon problem is a risk generated by a misperception of the problem.

Incrementalists would present the problem as being one of bells going out of tune, not as an acid rain problem. If some *ad hoc*, scientifically mysterious, local, temporary, partial solution is available, all well and good, for it can be employed in far less time and at far less expense than science can uncover the causes of the phenomenon. Suppose that a layer of grease were laid over the bells as a remedy: it could be tried and tested in a couple of years in controlled experiments. If this did not work, all that would have been lost is a few pennies' worth of grease and a year or two of bells continuing to go out of tune, after which some other quick and cheap solution might be tried. Indeed, many may be tested at the same time. Should the grease remedy be successful, it is likely to be so only to a limited extent and perhaps only locally, but a partial solution is better than none, especially one which can be improved empirically, using different greases, different ways of applying them, and so on, quickly and inexpensively. Learning about the ability of grease to stop the loss of tuning in bells by trial and error is far quicker and far less costly than learning how sulphur dioxide emissions affect tuning. If expensive filters were built on the chimneys of local boilers to remove the sulphur dioxide at source, for example, not only would this take many years, but it would prove a huge mis-investment if it turned out to have no beneficial effect on the problem of the bells. To put the matter a little more formally: decisions about *ad hoc* remedies such as greasing the bells have a low error cost, making policy insensitive to the conjecture that greasing will ameliorate the tuning problem. On the other hand, controlling sulphur dioxide emissions has a very high error cost, making that policy highly sensitive to the conjecture that the tuning problem is caused by acid rain. Seeking solutions like the former is a recognition that policy cannot be made to rest upon scientific conjectures such as those about acid rain.

Science and Policy—An Unhappy Marrige

It is a commonplace in the extensive literature on the relationship between science and policymaking that more and more decisions have to be made with a scientific element to them, that policymaking is increasingly concerned with technical issues. Two sources of this fashion seem to be important: people show an increasing willingness to couch the case in support of their favoured option in scientific terms, and scientific research itself throws up more and more issues for the attention of policymakers—what Schmandt (1984) calls 'scientific regulation'. The great success of the chemical industry since the Second World War has necessitated the control of many hundreds of potentially hazardous substances in the workplace and beyond in the general environment, as the growth in pharmaceutical products has required similar intensive regulation. During this period, concern for the environment has grown, adding to the technical nature of much policymaking. The assumption throughout the literature is that there are very special new problems caused by the need for policy to consider such increasingly technical issues. For example, in reviewing an extensive literature and before developing a number of studies to support their sceptical views, Hammond *et al.* (1983, p. 287) state that, 'Although the will to improve the use of scientific information in public policymaking does not seem to be lacking . . ., no satisfactory method for achieving this aim has yet been developed. Results of even the most dedicated attempts to improve such use . . . are widely regarded as having been disappointing.'

The same conclusion is reached in the special edition of *Science, Technology and Human Values* (1984) devoted to regulation and science.

But perhaps the problem is one of perception more than of reality. After all, what is the difference between settling a dispute over the control of an industrial chemical, where the workers appeal to scraps of scientific evidence supporting their view that it is poisonous, with the management denying this, and making policy on a matter far-removed from science—say, subsidies for farmers? Farmers will support their case by threats of food shortages in poor harvests, and opponents of the subsidy will deny the link, perhaps arguing that food imports could always prevent serious shortages of food at home. There is no time to settle the factual claims of the two parties, indeed they cannot be settled because there will always be an argument about whatever claims might be made in their support. Policy is therefore made by compromise, giving the farmers some of the subsidies they demand, but not all. Nor is there any way of checking that the policy has the desired outcome. If food production is increased by subsidies, this will be masked so efficiently by changes in weather, farming techniques and crops grown, that there will no way of picking out the effect of policy. Should there be no subsidy and should food shortages occur, there will be no way of knowing whether things would have been the least bit better had the alternative policy been implemented. Other agents who fear that their interests are threatened by the farming policy can enter the arena, urging a change in the policy itself, or can take some action to ameliorate its ill effects. Farm labour unions might, for example, attack subsidies to farmers if these appeared to lead to greater mechanization of farms, resulting in job losses, or they might fight for a wage subsidy themselves. This little story is utterly routine: its like could be told a thousand times a day in every country.

Now consider the more technical case of action taken to control a chemical hazard in the workplace. Evidence for and against the chemical's toxicity will be expounded by the workers, who seek its complete elimination, and by management, who want to keep things as they are, but no consensus is possible, as the over-critical model shows. In any case, there is neither money nor time to wait for a scientific consensus even if it were possible. A decision is therefore made by a compromise between the actors, perhaps banning the chemical for some uses but not others, or reducing its concentration to a half or one-third of existing levels. Should the policy work, any improvement in the health of the workers is almost certain to remain hidden, obscured by changes in the workers' eating and smoking habits, or general lifestyle, and by changes in the work-force itself. Failure is likely to be just as impenetrable, the deterioration in workers' health being masked in the same way. If other actors feel that their interests will suffer from whatever compromise is effected, they may try to alter the policy directly, or seek other ways of remedying their problem. The manufacturer of the chemical, for example, may support the case of the plant's managers that the chemical is safe, or may seek new markets for the product.

In reality, there is no difference at all between the two cases. But in terms of perception and expectations there is every difference. Our expectations about science are outraged in the second case: we are convinced that science ought to do better than this in informing policy. The answer is not to undertake some root-and-branch reform of the policy process, so that it can better utilize the discoveries of science, nor to seek for fundamental changes in the conduct of scientific research which would make its products more acceptable to policy-makers; rather, our expectations must be adjusted to what science can really deliver to the decision-making process. It is to this end that the present book is dedicated. Cases like that of the chemical hazard in the factory are systematically misperceived. Behind the claims and counter-claims of the workers and managers, locked in an inevitable clash of interests, stands science, neutral, objective, detached, disinterested, and therefore able to elevate policymaking beyond the mean squabble for political advantage where it has stood since before the stone age. When the inherent limitations on the use of science in decision-making which this book has laboured to elaborate are recognized, then perception must change. Misperception of the power of science is buttressed by the myth of rationality which looks to science as the provider of the information needed for efficient policymaking, whose influence is clear in the all too ordinary case of the Dutch bells discussed above. Without a moment's reflection, the solution to the problem of the bells' loss of tune is taken to involve the discovery of its causes through the application of scientific method. If such traps can be avoided, then policy involving technical issues can be seen to be the same in all essential respects as decision-making on any other kind of issue—which is the message of Chapter 7—describing how policy on the control of lead in Britain has been made in exactly the same way as policy on anything anywhere else.

But the story of misperception does not end here. Brickman (1984) has compared the use of science in policymaking in the United States and Western Europe, arguing that the extreme fragmentation and openness of American policymaking provides political actors with a much more severe problem of legitimating their power, for which reason science is often looked to lend political judgements an aura of objective authority. Policymaking in Europe, by contrast, generally involves bureaucratic actors who have adequate authority to suppress expressions of dissent in terms of constant bickering about the adequacy of the evidence on which their decisions are made. Committees of technical researchers and representatives of groups affected by the policy can therefore freely mix technical and political considerations as their discussions develop, and such groups are often very influential. Only the briefest statement of technical evidence generally needs to be made in support of policy decisions, unlike in the United States where a published scientific case can be crucial in gaining credibility. The openness of the American political system, however, ensures that the opposition can attack the technical case, no matter how sophisticated, painstaking and thorough, often employing their own experts. The present work underlines Brickman's realization that the role allotted to science in American policymaking is one which it simply cannot fulfil. Huge resources are wasted in the production of technical tomes, and grave delays in policymaking occur in the gestation period. Worse, the political process is distorted, the real questions at issue remaining undebated and hidden while arguments go on between a handful of qualified experts over minute technical points. Neither policymaking nor science acquire any credit from this double substitution of technical issues for political ones, and of experts for the real political actors. Science cannot provide the sort of legitimacy which actors in the policy drama so crave, and its inevitable failures weaken the political process as much as they lower the general standing of science in the wider community.

Bibliography

Ashby, E. and Anderson, M. (1981), *The Politics of Clean Air*, Oxford, Oxford University Press.

Bartlett, F. (1948), 'Challenges to Experimental Psychology', *Proceedings of the 12th International Congress of Psychology*, Edinburgh, Oliver and Boyd, pp. 23–30.

Blackburn, J. (1945), *Psychology and the Social Pattern*, London, Kegan Paul.

Blackburn, J. (1947), *The Framework of Human Behaviour*, London, Routledge and Kegan Paul.

Blackwell, A. (1943), 'A List of Researches in Educational Psychology and Teaching Method Presented for Higher Degree of British Universities 1918–1943', *British Journal of Educational Psychology*, **13–15**.

Block, N. and Dworkin, G. (1974), 'I.Q.: Heritability and Inequality, *Philosophy and Public Affairs*', **3**, pp. 331–407; **4**, pp. 40–9.

Block, N. and Dworkin, G. (1977), *The I.Q. Controversy*, London, Quartet.

Board of Education (1924), Consultative Committee Report, *Psychological Tests of Educable Capacity and Their Possible Use in the Public System of Education*, London, HMSO.

Board of Education (1926), Consultative Committee Report, *The Education of the Adolescent*, London, HMSO.

Board of Education (1931), Consultative Committee Report, *The Primary School*, London, HMSO.

Board of Education (1938), Consultative Committee Report, *Secondary Education With Special Reference to Grammar Schools and Technical High Schools*, London, HMSO.

Bodmer, W. (1972), 'Race and I.Q.—The Genetic Background', in K. Richardson (ed.), *Race Culture and Intelligence*, Harmondsworth, Penguin, reprinted A. Montague (ed.) (1975), *Race and I.Q.*, Oxford, Oxford University Press, pp. 252–86.

Boulding, K. (1964), Review of 'Strategy for Decision', *American Sociological Review*, **29**, p. 933.

Bowles, S. and Gintis, H. (1976), *Schooling in Capitalist America*, London, Routledge and Kegan Paul.

Bradford Hill, A. (1965), 'The Environment and Disease: Association or Causation?', *Proceedings of the Royal Society of Medicine*, pp. 295–300.

Braybrooke, D. and Lindblom, C. (1963), *A Strategy of Decision*, London, Collier Macmillan.

Brickman, R. (1984), 'Science and the Politics of Toxic Chemical Regulation—U.S. and European Contrasts', *Science, Technology and Human Values*, **9**, pp. 107–11.

British Medical Journal (1957), editorial, 'Dangers of Cigarette Smoking', **1**, pp. 1518–20.

British Medical Journal (1976), editorial, 'The Lethal Weed', **2**, p. 1522.

Brooks, H. (1984), 'The Resolution of Technically Intensive Public Policy Disputes', *Science, Technology and Human Values*, **9**, pp. 39–50.

Brown, H. (1977), 'Speech on the Occasion of the Dedication of the Stennis Center, Starkville, Mississippi State University, 21 October, quoted in D. Brewer, 'Where the Twain Meet, Reconciling Science and Politics in Analysis', *Policy Sciences*, **13**, (1981), pp. 269–79.

Burch, P. (1974), 'Does Smoking Cause Lung Cancer?', *New Scientist*, **61**, pp. 458–63.

Burch, P. (1978a), 'Smoking and Health', letter, *British Medical Journal*, **1**, p. 165.

Burch, P. (1978b), 'Smoking and Lung Cancer: The Problem of Inferring Cause', *Journal of the Royal Statistical Society*, **A141**, pp. 437–58.

Burt, C. (1917), *The Distribution and Relation of Educational Abilities*, London, King and Son.

Camhis, M. (1979), *Planning Theory and Philosophy*, London, Tavistock.

Cancro, R. (ed.) (1971), *Intelligence: Genetic and Environmental Influences*, New York, Grune and Stratton.

Caplan, N., Morrison, A. and Stambaugh, R. (1975), *The Use of Social Science Knowledge in Policy Decisions*, Ann Arbor, University of Michigan Press.

Carley, M. (1980), *Rational Techniques in Policy Making*, London, Heinemann.

Chambers, E. (1943), 'Statistics in Psychology and the Limitations of the Test Method', *British Journal of Psychology*, **33**, pp. 189–99.

Clark, I. (1974), 'Expert Advice in the Controversy about Supersonic Transport in the U.S.', *Minerva*, **12**, pp. 416–32.

Collingridge, D. (1980), *The Social Control of Technology*, London, Frances Pinter.

Collingridge, D. (1982), *Critical Decision Making*, London, Frances Pinter.

Collingridge, D. (1984a), *Technology in the Policy Process—Controlling Nuclear Power*, London, Frances Pinter.

Collingridge, D. (1984b), 'Criticizing Preferences', *Philosophy*, **59**, pp. 231–41.

Collingridge, D. and Douglas, J. (1984), 'Three Models of Policymaking: Expert Advice in the Control of Environmental Lead', *Social Studies of Science*, **14**, pp. 343–70.

Collins, H. (1975), 'The Seven Sexes: A Study in the Sociology of a Phenomenon, or the Replication of Experiments in Physics', *Sociology*, **9**, pp. 205–24.

Collins, H. (1981), 'Son of Seven Sexes: The Social Destruction of a Physical Phenomenon', *Social Studies of Science*, **11**, pp. 37–62.

Commission of the European Communities (1977), *Progress Report on the Implementation of the Council Directive on Biological Screening of the Population for Lead, (Directive 77/312/ EEC, of 29th March 1977)*, COM (81) 88 final, Brussels, 10 March 1981.

Conservation Society, 'Lead or Health', London, 1980.

Crompton, C. (1978), *The Cambridge School—The Life, Work and Influence of James Ward, W. Rivers, C. Myers and F. Bartlett*, Ph.D. thesis, University of Edinburgh.

Department of the Environment (1976), *Pollution Control in Great Britain, How it Works*, London, HMSO.

Department of the Environment (1977a), *Lead in Drinking Water*, Pollution Paper **12**, London, HMSO.

Department of the Environment (1977b), *Environmental Standards: A Description of UK Practice*, London, HMSO.

Department of Health and Social Security (1980), *Lead and Health*, London, HMSO.

Dobzhansky, T. (1973), *Genetic Diversity and Human Equality*, New York, Basic Books.

Doll, R. (1972), 'Smoking and Health', letter, *The Lancet*, **1**, p. 322.

Doll, R. (1974), 'Smoking, Lung Cancer and Occam's Razor', *New Scientist*, **61**, pp. 463–7.

Doll, R. and Hill, A. (1950), 'Smoking and Carcinoma of the Lung', *British Medical Journal*, **2**, pp. 739–48.

Doll, R. and Hill, A. (1952), 'A Study of the Aetiology of Carcinoma of the Lung', *British Medical Journal*, **2**, pp. 1271–86.

Doll, R. and Hill, A. (1956), 'Lung Cancer and Other Causes of Death in Relation to Smoking', *British Medical Journal*, **2**, pp. 1071–81.

Doll, R. and Hill, A. (1964), 'Mortality in Relation to Smoking: 10 Years' Observations of British Doctors', *British Medical Journal*, **1**, pp. 1399–410, 1460–7.

Doll, R. and Peto, R. (1976), 'Mortality in Relation to Smoking: 20 Years' Observations of British Doctors', *British Medical Journal*, **2**, pp. 1525–36.

Doty, P. (1972), 'Can Investigations Improve Scientific Advice— The Case of the ABM', *Minerva*, **10**, pp. 280–94.

Doyle, D. C. (1979), *Aspects of the Institutionalisation of British Psychology: The National Institute of Industrial Psychology 1921–39*, Ph.D. thesis, University of Manchester.

Dror, Y. (1964), 'Muddling through—Science or Inertia?', *Public Administration Review*, **24**, pp. 153–7.

Edwards, K. (1980), *Control of Environmental Lead Pollution*, Ph.D. thesis, Birmingham, University of Aston.

Elwood, P. (1983), 'The Lead Debate', Institution of Environmental Health Officers, 100th Environmental Health Congress, 5–8 September, Brighton, Sussex.

Elwood, P. and Gallacher, P. (1984), 'Lead in Petrol and Levels of Lead in Blood; Scientific Evidence and Social Policy', *Journal of Epidemiology and Community Health*, **38**, pp. 315–18.

Environmental Protection Agency (US) (1972), *Health Hazards of Lead*, Washington, DC, EPA.

Environmental Protection Agency (US) (1973a), *EPA's Position on the Health Effects of Airborne Lead*, Washington DC, EPA.

Environmental Protection Agency (US) (1973b), *EPA's Position on the Health Implications of Airborne Lead*, Washington DC, EPA.

Environmental Protection Agency (US) (1977), *Air Quality Criteria for Lead*, EPA—600/8-77/-17, Washington DC, EPA.

Ethyl Corporation (1972), *Comments on EPA's Proposed Lead Regulations*, New York, Ethyl Corporation.

Ethyl Corporation (1973), *Critique of 'EPA's Position on the Health Effects of Lead'*, New York, Ethyl Corporation.

Etzioni, A. (1967), Mixed Scanning; A 3rd Approach to Decision Making, *Public Administration Review*, **27**, pp. 385–92, reprinted, A. Faludi (ed.), *A Reader in Planning Theory*, Oxford, Pergamon, pp. 217–29.

Etzioni, A. (1968), *The Active Society*, New York, Free Press.

Eysenck, H. (1960), 'Smoking and Lung Cancer', *New Scientist*, **7**, p. 1559.

Eysenck, H. (1971), *Race, Intelligence and Education*, London, Temple Smith.

Eysenck, H. (1973), *The Inequality of Man*, London, Temple Smith.

Eysenck, H. (1980), *The Causes and Effects of Smoking*, London, Temple Smith.

Eysenck, H. and Kamin, L. (1981), *Intelligence, The Battle for the Mind*, London, Macmillan.

Eysenck, H., Tarrant, M., Woolf, M. and England, L. (1960), 'Smoking and Personality', *British Medical Journal*, **1**, pp. 1456–60.

Ezrahi, Y. (1976), 'The Jensen Controversy—Ethics and Politics of Knowledge in a Democracy' in C. Frankel (ed.), *Controversies in Social Science and Public Policy*, N.Y., Sage, pp. 149–70.

Fallows, S. (1979), 'The Nuclear Waste Disposal Controversy', in D. Nelkin (ed.), *Controversy*, Beverly Hills and London, Sage, pp. 87–110.

Fisher, R. (1958), 'Lung Cancer and Cigarettes?', letter, *Nature*, **182**, p. 108 and 'Dangers of Cigarette Smoking', letter, *Nature*, **182**, p. 108.

Fletcher, C. (1972), 'Smoking and Health', letter, *The Lancet*, **1**, p. 386.

Floud, J., Halsey A. and Martin F. (1956), *Social Class and Educational Opportunity*, London, Heinemann.

Ford, J. (1969), *Social Class and the Comprehensive*, London, Routledge and Kegan Paul.

Friedman, M. (1975), *Public Policy and the Smoking–Health Controversy*, Lexington, Mass., Lexington Books.

Frisby, J. (1969), *The History of Educational Psychology Teaching in English Training Colleges*, M.Ed. thesis, University of Nottingham.

Geminus (1960a), 'It Seems to Me', *New Scientist*, **7**, p. 1419.

Geminus (1960b), 'It Seems to Me', *New Scientist*, **7**, p. 1559.

Gershuny, J. (1978), 'Policy Making Rationality: A Reformulation', *Policy Sciences*, **9**, pp. 295–316.

Gillespie, B., Eva, D. and Johnston, R. (1979), 'Carcinogenic Risk Assessment in US and UK—The Case of Aldrin/Dieldrin, *Social Studies of Science*, **9**, pp. 265–301.

Gottesman, I. (1968), 'Biogenics of Race and Class' in M. Deutsch, I. Katz and A. Jensen (eds), *Social Class, Race and Psychological Development*, New York, Rinehart and Winston, pp. 11–51.

Gumbert, E. and Spring, J. (1974), *The Superschool and the Superstate—American Education in the 20th Century 1918–1970*, New York, Wiley.

Habermas, J. (1971), *Towards a Rational Society*, London, Heinemann.

Hadden, S. (1977), 'Technical Advice in Policy Making. A Propositional Inventory', in J. Harberer (ed.), *Science and Technology Policy*, Lexington, Mass., Lexington Books.

Hadden, S. (1979), 'DES and the Assessment of Risk' in D. Nelkin (ed.), *Controversy*, Beverly Hills and London, Sage, pp. 111–24.

Halsey, A. and Gardner, L. (1953), 'Selection for Secondary Education', *British Journal of Sociology*, **4**, pp. 60–75.

164 Bibliography

Hammond, K., Mumpower, J., Dennis, R., Fitch, S. and Crumpacker, W. (1983), 'Fundamental Obstacles to the Use of Scientific Information in Public Policy Making', *Technological Forecasting and Social Change*, **24**, pp. 287–97.

Handler, P. (1975), interview, *Wall Street Journal*, 3 April, p. 12.

Hansard (1978a), *Hansard*, **960**, 12 December.

Hansard (1978b), *Hansard*, **955**, 1 August.

Harvey, W. (1981), 'Plausibility and the Evaluation of Knowledge, A Case Study of Experimental Quantum Mechanics', *Social Studies of Science*, **11**, pp. 95–130.

Harwood, J. (1976), 'The Race–Intelligence Controversy—A Sociological Approach I', *Social Studies of Science*, **6**, pp. 369–94.

Harwood, J. (1977), 'The Race–Intelligence Controversy—A Sociological Approach II', *Social Studies of Science*, **7**, pp. 1–30.

Hearnshaw, L. (1964), *A Short History of British Psychology 1840–1950*, London, Methuen.

Hearnshaw, L. (1979), *Cyril Burt—Psychologist*, London, Hodder and Stoughton.

Heim, A. (1954), *The Appraisal of Intelligence*, London, Methuen.

Hirsch, J. (1971),'Behaviour—Genetic Analysis and Its Biosocial Consequences' in R. Cancro (ed.) (1971), *Intelligence: Genetic and Environmental Influences*, New York, Grune and Stratten, pp. 88–106, reprinted N. Block and G. Dworkin (eds) (1977), *The IQ Controversy*, London, Quartet, pp. 156–78.

Holcomb, R. (1970), 'Radiation Risks: A Scientific Problem?', *Science*, **167**, 6 February, pp. 853–5.

Hyman, J. (1969), letter, *New Republic*, **161**, pp. 30–1.

Jarratt, C. (1977), Parliamentary Expenditure Committee, *1st Report Session 1976–7, Preventive Medicine, Vol. III, Minutes of Evidence*, London, HMSO, p. 582.

Jencks, C., Smith, M., Ackland, H., Bane, M. Cohen, D. and Gintis, H. (1972), *Inequality. A Reassessment of the Effect of Family and Schooling in America*, New York, Basic Books.

Jensen, A. (1969), 'How Much Can We Boost I.Q. and Scholastic Achievement?', *Harvard Educational Review*, **39**, pp. 1–123, reprinted A. Jensen (ed.) (1972), *Genetics and Education*, London, Methuen.

Jensen, A. (ed.) (1972), *Genetics and Education*, London, Methuen.

Jensen, A. (1973), *Educability and Group Differences*, London, Methuen.

Jensen, A. (1975a), 'The Meaning of Heritability in Behavioural Science', *Educational Psychology*, **11**, pp. 171–83.

Jensen, A. (1975b), 'Race and Mental Ability', in F. Ebling (ed.), 'Racial Variation in Man', Institute of Biology Symposium 22, London, Blackwell, reprinted A. Halsey (ed.) (1977), *Heredity and Environment*, London, Methuen, pp. 215–62.

Jensen, A. (1980), *Bias in Mental Testing*, London, Methuen.

Jensen, A. (1981a), *Straight Talk About Mental Tests*, London, Methuen.

Jensen, A. (1981b), 'Obstacles, Problems and Pitfalls in Differential Psychology' in S. Scarr, *Race, Social Class and Individual Differences*, Hillsdale, New Jersey, Lawrence Erlbaum, pp. 483–513.

Jinks, J. and Fulker, D. (1970), 'Comparison of the Biometrical Genetical MAVA and Classical Approaches to the Analysis of Human Behaviour', *Psychological Bulletin*, **73**, pp. 311–49.

Kamin, L. (1974), *The Science and Politics of I.Q.*, Potomac, Maryland, Lawrence Erlbaum.

Kamin, L. (1981), Commentary in S. Scarr, *Race, Social Class and Individual Differences in I.Q.*, Hillsdale, New Jersey, Lawrence Erlbaum, pp. 467–82.

Karrier, C. (1972), 'Testing for Order and Control in the Corporate Liberal State', *Educational Theory*, **22**, pp. 154–70, 172–6, 178–80, reprinted in N. Block and G. Dworkin (eds) (1977), *The I.Q. Controversy*, London, Quartet Books, pp. 339–82.

Kazamias, A. (1966), *Politics, Society and Secondary Education in England*, Pennsylvania, University of Pennsylvania Press.

Knopp, C. (1979), 'The Origin of the American Scientific Debate Over Fallout Hazards', *Social Studies of Science*, **9**, pp. 403–22.

Kuhn, T. (1970), , 2nd edn, Chicago, University of Chicago Press.

Lakatos, I. (1970), 'Falsification and the Methodology of Scientific Research Programmes' in I. Lakatos and A. Musgrave (1970), *Criticism and the Growth of Knowledge*, Cambridge, Cambridge University Press, pp. 91–196, reprinted I. Lakatos (1978), *The Methodology of Scientific Research Programmes*, Cambridge, Cambridge University Press, pp. 8–101.

Lancet, The (1971), editorial, 'Counterblast to Tobacco', **1**, pp. 69–70.

Laski, H. (1931), *The Limitations of the Expert*, Fabian Tract **235**, London, Fabian Society.

Layzer, D. (1972), 'Science or Superstition?', *International Journal of Cognitive Psychology*, **1**, pp. 265–99, reprinted in N. Block and G. Dworkin (eds) (1977), *The I.Q. Controversy*, London, Quartet, pp. 194–241.

Layzer, D. (1974), 'Heritability Analysis of I.Q. Scores', *Science*, **183**, (4131), pp. 1259–66.

Lewontin, R. (1970), 'Race and Intelligence', *Bulletin of the Atomic Scientists*, **26**, pp. 2–8, reprinted N. Block and G. Dworkin (eds) (1977), *The I.Q. Controversy*, London, Quartet, pp. 78–92.

Lewontin, R. (1974), 'The Analysis of Variance and the Analysis of Cause', *American Journal of Human Genetics*, **26**, pp. 400–11, reprinted in N. Block and G. Dworkin (eds) (1977), *The I.Q. Controversy*, London, Quartet, pp. 179–93.

Lewontin, R. (1976), 'The Fallacy of Biological Determinism', *The Sciences*, pp. 6–10.

Li, C. (1971), 'A Tale of Two Thermos Bottles', in R. Cancro (ed.), *Intelligence; Genetic and Environmental Influences*, New York, Grune and Stratton, pp. 162–84.

Lindblom, C. (1965), *The Intelligence of Democracy*, London, Collier Macmillan.

Lindblom, C. (1968), *The Decision Making Process*, Englewood Cliffs, NJ, Prentice Hall.

Lindblom, C. (1979), 'Still Muddling Not Yet Through', *Public Administration Review*, **39**, pp. 517–26.

Lippmann, W. (1922–3), 'The Mental Age of Americans', 'The Mystery of the "A" Men', 'The Reliability of Intelligence Tests', 'The Abuses of the Tests', 'Tests of Hereditarian Intelligence', 'A Future for the Tests', 'The Great Confusion', letter to *New Republic*, all reprinted in N. Block and G. Dworkin (eds) (1977), *The I.Q. Controversy*, London, Quartet Books.

Macleod, I. (1954), *House of Commons Debate* **523**, Written Answers, 12 February, Cols. 173–4.

Mazur, A. (1973), 'Disputes Between Experts', *Minerva*, **11**, pp. 243–62.

Medawar, P. (1977), 'Are I.Q's Nonsense?', *New York Review*, **24**, pp. 13–18.

Medical Research Council (1957), 'Tobacco Smoking and Cancer of the Lungs', *British Medical Journal*, **1**, pp. 1523–4.

Metallic Contamination Sub-Committee on Lead (1951), *Report*, Ministry of Food Bulletin No. 628, London, HMSO.

Ministry of Agriculture, Fisheries and Food (1975), *Food Additives and Contaminants Committee's Review of the Lead in Food Regulations, 1961*, London, HMSO.

Ministry of Health (1963), *On The State of the Public Health*, Annual Report of the Chief Medical Officer, London, HMSO.

Morris, N. (1961), 'An Historian's View of Examinations', in S. Wiseman (ed.) (1961), *Examinations and English Education*. Manchester, Manchester University Press.

Morton, N. (1972), 'Human Behavioural Genetics' in L. Ehrman,

G. Omenn and E. Caspari (eds), *Genetics, Environment and Behaviour*, New York, Academic Press, pp. 247–65.

Mulkay, M. (1979), *Science and the Sociology of Knowledge*, London, George Allen and Unwin.

National Academy of Sciences (1921), *Psychology Examining in the US Army*, R. Yerkes (ed.), Vol. 15., Washington DC, NAS.

National Academy of Sciences (1971), *Lead in Perspective*, Washington DC, National Academy of Sciences.

National Research Council (US) (1980), *Lead in the Human Environment*, Washington DC, National Academy of Sciences.

Nature (1972), editorial, 'How Much of I.Q. is Inherited?', **240** (5376), p. 69.

Nelkin, D. (1971), *Nuclear Power and Its Critics*, Ithaca, Cornell University Press.

Nelkin, D. (1975), 'The Political Impact of Technical Expertise', *Social Studies of Science*, **5**, pp. 35–54.

Nelkin, D. (1979), Introduction to D. Nelkin (ed.), *Controversy*, Beverly Hills and London, Sage, pp. 14–18, reprinted in B. Barnes and D. Edge (1982), *Science in Context*, Milton Keynes, Open University Press pp. 276–81.

Newman, H., Freeman, F. and Holzinger, K. (1937), *Twins: A Study of Heredity and Environment*, Chicago, University of Chicago Press.

Nowotny, H. (1982), 'Experts in a Participatory Experiment—The Austrian Debate on Nuclear Energy', *Bulletin of Science, Technology and Society*, **2**, pp. 107–24.

Nowotny, H. (1984), 'Science for Public Policy, A New Branch of Science Inc.', International Institute for Applied System Analysis, Laxenburg, Austria, 16–20 January, forum *Science for Public Policy*.

Nowotny, H. and Hirsch, H. (1980), 'The Consequences of Dissent—Sociological Reflections on the Controversy of the Low Dose Effects', *Research Policy*, **9**, pp. 278–94.

Parliamentary Expenditure Committee (1977), *1st Report of the Expenditure Committee, Session 1976–77, Preventive Medicine, Vol. 1, Report*, London, HMSO.

Penrose, L. (1950), 'Paper to British Association for the Advancement of Science', *The Advancement of Science*, **6** (24), p. 357.

Peterson, J. and Markle, G. (1979), 'Politics and Science in the Laetrile Controversy', *Social Studies of Science*, **9**, pp. 139–66.

Peto, R. (1980), 'Smoking Report Under Fire Over Funds and Facts', London, *Sunday Times*, 14 December, p. 2.

Pickering, A. (1981), 'Constraints on Controversy: The Case of the Magnetic Monopole', *Social Studies of Science*, **11**, pp. 63–93.

Pickering, A. (1984), *Constructing Quarks*, Edinburgh, Edinburgh University Press.

Pinch, T. (1981), 'The Sun-Set: The Presentation of Certainty in Scientific Life', *Social Studies of Science*, **11**, pp. 131–58.

Polanyi, M. (1962), 'The Republic of Science', *Minerva*, **1**, pp. 54—73.

Popham, G. (1981), 'Government and Smoking, Policy Making and Pressure Groups', *Policy and Politics*, **9**, pp. 331–47.

Popper, K. (1959), *The Logic of Scientific Discovery*, London, Hutchinson.

Popper, K. (1969), 'Truth, Rationality and the Growth of Scientific Knowledge', in K. Popper (1969), *Conjectures and Refutations*, 3rd edn, London, Routledge and Kegan Paul, pp. 215–52.

Powell, E. (1962), *House of Commons Debate*, **655**, 12 March, Col. 888.

Priebe, P. and Kaufman, G. (1980), 'Making Government Policy Under Uncertainty—100yrs of Saccarine in Laboratory and Congress', *Minerva*, **18**, 556–74.

Ravetz, J. (1973), *Scientific Knowledge and Its Social Problems*, Harmondsworth, Penguin.

Reeve, C. (1985), *The Role of Experts in Policymaking*, Ph.D. thesis, University of Aston.

Rein, M. (1976), *Social Science and Public Values*, Harmondsworth, Penguin.

Reiser, J. (1966), 'Smoking and Health: Congress and Causality', in S. Lakoff (ed.), *Knowledge and Power*, New York, Free Press, pp. 293–311.

Robbins, D. and Johnston, R. (1976), 'The Role of Cognitive and Occupational Differentiation in Scientific Controversies', *Social Studies of Science*, **6**, pp. 349–68.

Royal College of Physicians (London) (1962), *Smoking and Health*, London, Pitman.

Royal College of Physicians (London) (1971), *Smoking and Health Now*, London, Pitman.

Royal College of Physicians (London) (1977), *Smoking or Health*, London, Pitman.

Rubinstein, D. and Simon, B. (1973), *The Evolution of the Comprehensive School 1926–1972*, London, Routledge and Kegan Paul (2nd edn.).

Russell, S. (1982), 'Risk Assessment as a Political Activity', *Working Paper*, Technology Policy Unit, University of Aston, Birmingham.

Scarr, S. (1981), *Race, Social Class and Individual Differences in I.Q.*, Hillsdale, New Jersey, Lawrence Erlbaum.

Schmandt, J. (1984), 'Regulation and Science', *Science, Technology and Human Values*, **9**, pp. 23–38.

Schulman, P. (1975), 'Non-Incremental Policymaking: Notes Towards an Alternative Paradigm', *American Political Science Review*, **69**, pp. 1354–70.

Self, P. (1974), 'Is Comprehensive Planning Possible and Rational?', *Policy and Politics*, **2**, pp. 193–203.

Seltzer, C. (1972a), Critical Appraisal of the Royal College of Physicians' Report, *The Lancet*, **1**, pp. 243–8.

Seltzer, C. (1972b), 'Smoking and Health', letter, *The Lancet*, **1**, p. 386.

Seltzer, C. (1974), 'Smoking and Cancer', letter, *New Scientist*, **62**, pp. 195–6.

Seltzer, C. (1978), Comments, *Journal of the Royal Statistical Society*, **A141**, pp. 463–4.

Sherlock, J., Evans, W., Hislop, J., Kay, J., Law, R., MacWeeny, D., Smart, G., Topping, G., and Wood, R. (1985), 'Analysis—Accuracy and Precision?', *Chemistry in Britain*, **21**, (11), pp. 1019–21.

Simon, B. (1953), *Intelligence Testing and the Comprehensive School*, London, Lawrence and Wishart, reprinted B. Simon (ed.) (1971), *Intelligence, Psychology and Education*, London, Lawrence Wishart, pp. 29–121.

Simon, B. (1967), 'Classification and Streaming—A Study of Grouping in English Schools 1860–1960', in P. Nash (ed.), *History and Education*, New York, reprinted B. Simon (1971), *Intelligence, Psychology and Education*, London, Lawrence Wishart, pp. 200–31.

Simon, B. (1974), *The Politics of Educational Reform 1920–40*, London, Lawrence Wishart.

Sutherland, G. (1977), The Magic of Measurement: Mental Testing and English Education 1900–1940, *Transactions, The Royal Historical Society*, **27**, pp. 135–53.

Sutherland, G. (1981), Measuring Intelligence: English Local Education Authorities and Mental Testing 1919–39, in C. Webster (ed.), *Biology Medicine and Society* Cambridge University Press, Cambridge, pp. 315–35.

Sutherland, G. and Sharp, S. (1980), The First Official Psychologist in the Wurrld, Aspects of the Professionalization of Psychology in Early 20th Century Britain, *History of Science*, **18**, pp. 181–208.

Tawney, R. (ed.) (1922), *Secondary Education or All—A Policy for Labour*, Allen and Unwin, London.

Taylor, H. (1980), *The I.Q. Game*, Brighton, Sussex, Harvester Press.

Thoday, J. (1969), 'Limitations to Genetic Comparisons of Populations', *Journal of Biosocial Science*, **1**, reprinted, N. Block and G. Dworkin (eds) (1977), *The I.Q. Controversy*, London, Quartet, pp. 131–45.

Thoday, J. (1973), 'Educability and Group Differences', *Nature*, **245**, reprinted, N. Block and G. Dworkin (eds) (1977), *The I.Q. Controversy*, London, Quartet, pp. 146–55.

Thompson, J. (1961), 'Co-operation Between Educational Psychologists and Sociologists', University of Leeds Institute of Education, *Researches and Studies*, **22** .

Thomson, R. (1968), *The Pelican History of Psychology*, Harmondsworth, Penguin.

Travis, G. (1981), 'Replicating Replication? Aspects of the Social Construction of Learning in Planarian Worm', *Social Studies of Science*, **11**, 11–32.

Vaughan-Morgan, J. (1957), *House of Commons Debate*, **572**, 27 June, Cols. 426–32.

Vernon, P. (1950), Paper to British Association for the Advancement of Science, *The Advancement of Science*, **6**, (24), p. 357.

Vernon, P. (ed.) (1957), *Secondary School Selection*.

Vernon, P. (1979), *Intelligence, Heredity and Environment*, Freeman, San Francisco.

Waldron, H. and Stöfen, D. (1974), *Sub-clinical Lead Poisoning*, Academic Press, London.

Weiss, C. (1977), Introduction in C. Weiss (ed.), *Using Social Research in Public Policy Making*, Heath, Lexington.

Weiss, C. (1982), 'Policy Research in the Context of Diffuse Decision Making', in D. Kallen, G. Kosse, H. Wagenaar, J. Kloprogge, and M. Vorbeck (eds.), *Social Science Research and Public Policy-Making—A Re-appraisal*, Windsor, UK, NFER-Nelson, pp. 288–314.

Weiss, C. and Bucuvalas, M. (1980), *Social Science Research and Decision Making*, New York, University of Columbia Press.

Wiseman, C. (1978), 'Selection of Major Planning Issues', *Policy Sciences*, **9**, pp. 71–86.

Zangwill, O. (1950), *An Introduction to Modern Psychology*, London, Methuen.

Index

3 1854 000 009 574

DATE DUE